Where no angels dwell

Air Vice-Marshal Sandy Johnstone CB DFC
with Roderick Grant

Where no angels dwell

Foreword by the Duke of Hamilton KT PC GCVO AFC

 JARROLDS

JARROLDS PUBLISHERS (LONDON) LTD
178–202 Great Portland Street, London W1

AN IMPRINT OF THE  HUTCHINSON GROUP

London Melbourne Sydney
Auckland Bombay Toronto
Johannesburg New York

★

First published 1969

*This book has been set in Imprint, printed in Great Britain
on Antique Wove paper, and bound by The Camelot Press Ltd
London and Southampton*

09 098710 1

*To all who served with
No. 602 (City of Glasgow) Squadron,
Auxiliary Air Force—
stout-hearted comrades both
in peace and in war*

Secure, serene; dumb now the night-hawk's threat;
The guns' low thunder drumming o'er the tide;
The anguish pulsing in her stricken side. . . .
All is at peace. . . . But, never, heart, forget:
For this her youngest, best, and bravest died,
These bright dews once were mixed with bloody sweat.

Walter de la Mare

Contents

Illustrations

Acknowledgements

Grateful thanks are due to Mr. Patrick Garrow, Public Relations Officer, Ministry of Defence (Air), for assistance during the early planning stages of this book; The Literary Trustees of Walter de la Mare and The Society of Authors as their representative for permission to reproduce an extract from Walter de la Mare's poem *Peace*; Mr. Morris Allan of *Photocraft*, Dunfermline, for permission to reproduce the photograph facing page 96; the Editor of the *Scottish Daily Express* for permission to reproduce the photograph of Rudolf Hess's crashed ME 110; the Editor of *The Scotsman* for permission to reproduce the photograph of the Shackleton facing page 97; His Grace the Duke of Hamilton, K.T., P.C., G.C.V.O., A.F.C., for providing an account of the arrival of Rudolf Hess in Britain; Mrs. Pat Balmer for typing the manuscript; and Mr. R. E. Field for assistance in compiling the Index.

Foreword

by His Grace the Duke of Hamilton,
KT PC GCVO AFC

It was not without a good deal of opposition that Lord Trenchard, who in 1918 became the first Chief of Air Staff of the Royal Air Force, started the Auxiliary Air Force in 1925. These squadrons, with a small nucleus of Regulars, were formed with the object of becoming front-line units. The opportunity soon seized the imagination of enterprising young men in all kinds of different jobs who proved that they were eagerly prepared to devote the major part of their spare time to learning and performing Air Force duties in their respective units.

Five squadrons were first formed: two in London, one in Edinburgh, one in Glasgow and one at Castle Bromwich, Birmingham. By 1939 these had been increased to twenty squadrons, all trained and ready for action. In these Auxiliary squadrons there was an atmosphere of enjoyment almost as if we were engaged in a game or sport, combined with a serious appreciation of the importance of our training in terms of the country's survival. It resulted in that particular combination of effort by air crew and all the ground crew trades that went to form a unit. The A.A.F. put in as much flying time as the regular R.A.F., achieving a high degree of operational skill so that when the war came squadrons manned their war stations as front-line units. It was, in fact, the Edinburgh and Glasgow Auxiliary squadrons that first went into action, shortly after the outbreak of war in 1939.

The part-time personnel served full time, but at the cessation of hostilities most of them returned to civilian jobs. The contribution that the Auxiliary Air Force played in the war was undeniably of great significance, although impossible to measure. For during the war, with ever-changing personnel, there eventually became little or no difference between Regular and Auxiliary squadrons. Three Auxiliary officers have now attained Air Rank, the present Chief of the Defence Staff is one of them, and another is the recent Air Officer Scotland and Northern Ireland, Air Vice-Marshal A. V. R. Johnstone.

For me this book recalls a particular day in 1934 when, as Commanding Officer of No. 602 Squadron, I had to interview an infectiously light-hearted and enthusiastic young man who was eager to join us. He was Sandy Johnstone, who was to become one of the squadron's most gallant members and successful war-time leaders.

Where No Angels Dwell is part of the history of flying by one who has a special story to tell because he himself played a notable part in it. For this reason, and for the sake of a very old friendship, I am indeed happy to have been given this opportunity to speed it on its way.

Preface

Collaborating with someone on the writing of a book is not always the easiest of tasks. Sometimes it involves two people of differing viewpoints; differing complexities of character; indeed, as in this case, different generations. When the work is in hand each has to lean on the other—talking, questioning, answering, guiding, sometimes arguing, but above all striving to mould into shape the creation that means so much to both: the book.

When I first met Air Vice-Marshal A. V. R. Johnstone, or as he prefers to be known, Sandy Johnstone, to discuss the possibilities of a book, he told me with the same air of modesty which I was later to appreciate as being characteristic: 'I doubt whether I have, in fact, a story worth telling.' Nevertheless the matter didn't end there and *Where No Angels Dwell* eventually emerged—the result of a series of meetings, endless conversations, tape-recordings, notes, letters, and even chats on the telephone.

An accident on the rugby field in 1934 turned Sandy Johnstone towards flying in his spare time and at weekends. He was seventeen when he joined No. 602 (City of Glasgow) Squadron, Auxiliary Air Force. Six years later, as a Squadron Leader, he was in command and leading his men into the grim and turbulent period of the Battle of Britain.

On September 11, 1940, he was awarded the D.F.C. By this time he had shot down four enemy aircraft. Later he was credited with a total of eight enemy aircraft plus four probable hits, and comments: 'I had a lot of luck and anyway I'm sure someone made a miscalculation.'

Sandy Johnstone was in Malta when the island battled for
its existence against tremendous odds in 1942; he was 'Opera-
tions 1' in the underground War Room at Bentley Priory in
Middlesex when the D-Day invasion took place; in Eire, as Air
Attaché after the war, he met Admiral Lord Mountevans—
Evans of the *Broke*—after he had been shipwrecked; with Aidan
Crawley, the then Under-Secretary of State for Air, he visited
the terrorist infested Malayan jungles when the Communist
Emergency was approaching its peak in 1950.

Later, in 1957, he helped to form the Royal Malayan Air
Force and, at the request of the Prime Minister, Tengku Abdul
Rahman, was made the first Chief of Air Staff with the rank of
Air Commodore. In November, 1963, he was flung head-long
into the break-up of the Rhodesian Federation and while in
Lusaka was fiercely criticized on a national radio broadcast by
the then Chief Minister, Kenneth Kaunda. In 1964 he was
again in the Far East as Commander of the Air Forces in
Borneo, during the tense period of confrontation between
Indonesia and Malaysia.

In 1966, by now a Companion of the Most Honourable Order
of the Bath, he was back in his native Scotland, an Air Vice-
Marshal in command of an area which had as its northernmost
limiting mark, the North Pole.

Sandy Johnstone has never been far away when history was
in the making, but *Where No Angels Dwell* is not solely concerned with him in this role. There have been many occasions
when even the most serious incident has had a funny side to it—
his keen sense of humour has always made him aware of this;
the comradeship that exists in the Royal Air Force, at all levels
of rank, is something he is never slow to acknowledge.

Since that Saturday afternoon in 1934 when he made his
first flight in an Avro 504 of World War I vintage he has never
lost his love of flying. When he retired he had piloted one
hundred and four different types of aircraft.

Even as an Air Vice-Marshal he was still eager to get behind
the controls of an aircraft just as, despite his high rank, his
obvious understanding of human nature kept him keenly aware

of the individual identities of the men who served under him.

As one airman told me: 'The Old Man—now he's what they mean when they talk about a real gentleman.'

Collaborating with someone like this on the writing of a book does ensure that the task is made a good deal easier.

Farnham, Surrey

RODERICK GRANT

1   Dilemma over Palestine

The fierce, fiery sun beat down mercilessly, turning the cramped cockpit into an oven of discomfort. Drops of sweat trickled down from my armpits and I felt rivulets of warm moisture running down my back to gather in pools at the waistband of my trousers. High above the Holy Land I slowly fried as my single-engined Fairey Fulmar nosed its ponderous way towards Haifa.

To the north the sudden cliff-like promontory of Mount Carmel rose up to dominate the landscape while to the east the Dead Sea stretched out like a great black sponge, shimmering in the intense heat.

Without warning, the Fulmar lurched and fell as she hit an air pocket. The suddenness of the violent movement threw me back in my seat, jerking my head forward. Only then, as I corrected the trim of the aircraft, did I realize that I had been almost asleep.

I shook my head in an effort to clear my brain but the muzziness remained and my eyelids started to droop once more. Then I smelt the fumes and for the first time realized that what air was left inside was filled with a sweet, sickly stench.

Quickly I pulled back the glass hood and with the burst of cool air came a stream of sticky fluid. It hit me in the face as if it had been thrown from a bucket and blinded me as surely as if a sack had been placed over my head. In my confusion I stood hard on one of the rudder bars and the Fulmar, her engine protesting loudly at the rough treatment, swung over on the port wing. With one hand I tried to wipe the oily film from the front of my goggles, while with the other I moved the stick over to put the aircraft on level flight again.

Even as the fresh air swirled around the cockpit I could smell the fumes growing stronger. The fluid continued to spray over me in great streams forced onwards by the fast-flowing slip stream. As it splattered off my flying suit it hit the controls and instruments. Everything I touched dripped with the foulness of dark, sticky oil.

As swiftly as I wiped the mess from my goggles it was replaced by more and in utter darkness I groped to keep control of the tough little Fulmar. But the steady stream of oil was making me heavy-handed and, as if in rebellion, the aircraft shuddered, sending a tremor running through the fuselage. The warning was plain.

My mind worked overtime. A smell like ether came to haunt my nostrils. If I shut the hood again I knew I would be overcome within minutes. If I kept the canopy open, how was I to see? The predicament was made even more complicated because of my passenger, Roy Clay. It was useless trying to get him to bale out. Although he was only several feet behind me in the rear cockpit the space between us was filled by the large main fuel tank. I could not see him, nor could he either see or hear me. Just as I was, he too was alone.

Globules of oil ran around my neck and tried to force their way into my flying suit. As I moved the stick over I felt my hand slip off the surface, now grown slippery and treacherous. There was only one course of action left—to get down on the ground as quickly as possible. The chances were that the aircraft would crash, but it was a risk that would have to be taken. It would not be my first crash. Wryly, beneath my oil-blackened face, I felt that it could very well be my last.

Still unable to see a thing, I gently eased the stick forward. The Fulmar obeyed and I felt the nose dip slightly . . .

It was June, 1942, and as a Wing Commander and Station and Sector Commander at Haifa, in Palestine, I had decided to pay a visit to some of the outlying airfields, accompanied by my senior operations officer, Roy Clay. To get around between these remote outposts I used a Fleet Air Arm two seater aircraft—a Fairy Fulmar, which was a development of the old and reliable 'Battle'. Although normally a pleasant aircraft to fly, the Fulmar had not been fully tested for operations in hot climates and troubles were constantly developing in the hydraulic systems owing to the pipe lines bursting when the fluid inside expanded in the heat. My own aircraft had experienced this trouble on a couple of occasions.

The first part of our journey to Abukir, near Alexandria, was uneventful and after a tour of inspection we set off again on the return flight via Ismailia, in Egypt, and Kalundia, a small landing strip on the outskirts of Jerusalem.

As the Fulmar droned on across the Nile Delta everything was serene. The engine roared away powerfully, never missing a stroke and all the dashboard instruments were reading correctly. The sun blazed down from a clear blue sky and as I started to circle the airfield at Ismailia I could see great tracts of barren desert baking in the heat. Lining up the aircraft for my approach I had a perfect view of the long stretch of desert which had been levelled out some years previously to give an added take-off run to a flight of Wellesleys, making their successful bid for the world's long distance record by flying from Egypt to Cape Darwin, in Australia, non-stop in 1937. This piece of extra runway had not been used since and was now covered with sand.

As Ismailia was a large airfield with a splendid, long runway, without the extra piece, I brought the Fulmar in with plenty of speed in reserve. Down . . . down . . . down she went until I felt the wheels brush the runway about one-third of the way along its normal length. Steadily increasing the pressure, I applied the brake lever. Nothing happened. The Fulmar pressed onwards along the rock hard surface without any appreciable difference in speed.

I pumped furiously on the brake lever but it felt loose and slack. Obviously the hydraulic system had given out again, leaving me without any brakes to halt the Fulmar's progress. The aircraft must have been touching 50 miles per hour as we flashed past the outer dispersal area and on to the final 'long distance' stretch. Careering on, I could see the end of the strip quite plainly when the Fulmar struck a slight bump in the otherwise smooth surface. At once she began to slacken speed and I blessed the fact that little repair work had been carried out on this stretch over the years. The rise in the ground had been enough to slow the momentum and gradually the speed dropped to a mere crawl. With feet to go before the runway joined forces with the desert again the Fulmar came to a stop.

The workshops at Ismailia weren't long in carrying out repairs and after a few hours' rest Roy and I set off for Kalundia. The airstrip there, so far as size was concerned, was the complete opposite of the one from which we had just taken off. Good wheel brakes were essential for a landing and as I touched down I prayed silently that there would be no repeat of the previous performance. However, the system did not fail this time and we were able to reach the watch office without having to have a car sent out into the desert to fetch us.

But problems were not to remain hidden and dormant for long. The Fulmar for all its pleasantness in flight, was under-powered for a take-off such as had to be made from this small landing strip. Because of the wind direction it was necessary to take off uphill across the main Jerusalem–Nablus road. The boundaries of the airfield were clearly marked by old oil drums, painted in vivid orange and black colours, and a local policeman was summoned to stop oncoming traffic in preparation for our take-off.

Yet again I wished Roy a pleasant flight as he climbed into his eyrie behind the fuel tank. I scrambled up and got into my seat and started up. Taxying as far to the leeward end of the strip as I could reach without running into really rough country I faced the Fulmar into the wind and 'gave her the gun'.

The aircraft took an age to pick up speed but by the time we crossed the road she had ceased to trundle along like some ancient hand-cart and had developed some power. As we crossed the highway two grey painted buses were drawn up, each packed to capacity, and rows of Arab and Jewish faces peered out of the windows to watch our efforts. What a show they must have had!

Fortunately, the hop across the roadway started the Fulmar bouncing up and down and I thought there could now be no difficulty in getting airborne. How wrong I was. By the time we had reached the end of the strip the Fulmar still would not lift off. The aircraft continued to bounce merrily and on one occasion it was well-timed. As we passed the boundary a row of orange and black oil drums faced us ominously. Like a racehorse the Fulmar rose, passed over the tops with inches to spare, then was down on hard earth again. I tried putting on all the power in the stout little engine but to no avail.

In true pilot's jargon I was, by this time, 'committed to take-off'. To put it bluntly I had to get up in the air or end up in a heap somewhere in the distance. Up and down . . . up and down . . . went the Fulmar, by now on a slight incline. In this crazy fashion we hopped for around two hundred yards all the way to the top of the hill. At the summit she faltered momentarily as if faced by an enormous challenge. But, as the ground fell away in a mass of boulders and rubble the Fulmar decided that the fun was over. As if nothing had happened I felt the wheels lift off as the aircraft launched over the edge. For a few seconds there were several violent tremors throughout the fuselage—then we were climbing away and I brought her round to circle Kalundia before heading for Haifa.

Far down below I saw the two buses moving off along the road. No doubt there was plenty of chattering among the passengers as they discussed the spectacle which they had just watched.

It was only when I levelled out that I remembered Roy sitting in the rear. It was fortunate that I couldn't see his face—or hear him. It had been bad enough for me, but at least I knew what had been happening. Alone, with practically no visibility except to the side, Roy must have thought he was in the hands of some madman during our recent take-off. I decided to tell him the full story whenever we touched down, before he had any opportunities to get the first word in.

The Fulmar had been fitted with a communications system linking the two cockpits but whoever designed it had, I'm sure, never flown in his life. It consisted of a speaking tube arrangement through which it was difficult enough to distinguish what was being said with the engine off and utterly impossible when it was running. Because of the effect it had upon tempers we had long ceased to bother about it. Each man would sit alone with his own private thoughts for the duration of a flight. To the pilot this was no hardship because he had plenty to do, but for the passenger, flying in a Fulmar amounted to little more than an uncomfortable, boring experience. So far, I guessed that our particular flight had been uncomfortable for Roy but I doubted if he could call it boring. So much seemed to have happened unexpectedly.

It was extremely interesting to fly over Palestine as it was possible to distinguish old tracks leading to the hill-tops and often the traces of ancient dwellings which had doubtless been there since the days of Christ. Looking to the west and south it was possible to follow the coastline from where it arrived northwards from Egypt. In the distance I could see the modern white buildings of Tel Aviv reflected in the sunlight, contrasting strangely with the squalid Arab hovels of Jaffa—the two being virtually one and the same town.

To the north was Mount Carmel; to the east the Dead Sea. In between, the landscape alternated between desert and vast areas of scrub, littered with rocks. . . .

It was down into unfriendly terrain such as this that, blinded and saturated by oily fluid, I forced the Fulmar.

The experience of descending with my vision obliterated was similar to night flying. However, at least in the hours of darkness one could read the phosphorescent figures on the dials and be guided by the occasional star. But now the smell and the foulness of the oily liquid, still bubbling and pouring over me, put a different aspect on what I was attempting to do.

I shook my head and wiped frantically at my goggles, but it was no good. Something tickled my nose and I sneezed. As my mouth opened I felt a spray of oil rush in. Cursing, I spat out the muck but the taste remained to cling to my tongue and teeth.

Raising myself from the seat I tried to lean over the side of the cockpit and, as I lifted my goggles from my face, I found to my delight that I could both see and breathe freely in this position. For the moment my troubles were over, but for how long? I pondered.

During my period of blindness the Fulmar had descended about one thousand feet and I set about adjusting the trim and correcting the course. With the cool air lapping my face I peered down into the cockpit and scraped some of the filth from the compass. Before the liquid had time to cover it up again I got a reading and made the adjustment. It was then I discovered where the liquid was coming from.

In the initial shock of opening the hood and being hit in the face I had thought that the mess had been pouring in from the engine. Although it was still a problem, at least when it came to a landing, I found that the cause of the trouble was the beastly hydraulic system again. This time it had burst open inside the cockpit. With the hood open the whirling draught had acted in the same manner as a fountain, spraying the fluid upwards over my face and body.

The fact that it was the hydraulic system and not a leak from the engine accounted for the sweet smell. The fluid used in it contained a large proportion of ether. Had the Fulmar not lurched suddenly in an air pocket, common hazards over desert country, I might very well have drifted into a deep sleep. Under this anaesthetic I would have been deeply unconscious by the time she ran out of fuel—and faltered.

Leaning out over the side I peered down, looking for a suitable place to land. But as far as I could see there was nowhere large enough. It was either too hilly, or where there was a stretch of flat land, boulders and rocks were too numerous for comfort. Then I had the idea. If I was flying in this fashion just now, why not continue to Haifa in the same way—hanging half-in and half-out of the cockpit? Again, I repeated the performance of changing the course and as the wind plucked at my goggles, now placed over my forehead, and lifted some of the muck from my face, I flew on.

Gradually the force of the wind and the current became too much for my eyes. The glare of the sun burned into my pupils and forced me to screw my eyelids together to protect them. I solved this one by looking backwards for a couple of minutes then turning and staring for as long as I could to the front and side in order to take a sighting on any familiar landmarks.

In this crazy fashion I flew on with Roy only a few feet away, but, because of the shape of the fuselage, unable to see his pilot, half-out of the cockpit and flying the aircraft forward while looking to the rear!

The airfield at Haifa was reasonably large with plenty of runway. As I made my approach I saw several people on the ground staring up, shielding their eyes against the sun, and shouting to others at work to come and watch. To anyone down below it must have looked as if the pilot of the aircraft flying low overhead was attempting to climb out and jump overboard, without apparently there being anything wrong whatsoever.

The runway loomed nearer and nearer. I steeled myself against the blasting current as the time came to put the wheels on the strip. Twenty feet to go . . . fifteen . . . ten and then, as if everything was perfectly normal, the wheels gently touched the runway. We were down and, as if in triumph, the brakeless Fulmar charged along the strip in a final burst of speed. It was just as well the runway was fairly long because it took ages to bring her to a stop. Immediately, I clambered out and in a flash I heard the hood of Roy's cockpit slide open with a crash.

He stuck his head out, then his shoulders: 'What the hell do you think you're doing? I've never . . .'

His shouting stopped abruptly and his mouth hung open in astonishment as he saw his Commanding Officer standing covered from head to foot in foul, greasy liquid. I'm sure I must have looked as miserable and awful as I felt.

He jumped on to the runway. 'What happened? Where did all that stuff come from?'

In the distance I saw a staff car speeding towards us, a cloud of thick dust rising in its wake.

I gave the fuselage of the sturdy Fulmar a resounding thump with the palm of my hand. 'Well, Roy, you remember when we took off from Kalundia we had to bump over some rough ground . . .'

The look on his face told me that he remembered only too well!

2 Up, up and away

Had it not been for an accident at school, followed later by a coincidence, I might never have taken up flying. During my last year at Kelvinside Academy, in Glasgow, I injured my left leg while playing for my School Rugby XV. While in the middle of a particularly tough scrum I found myself being pinned on the ground with my left leg jutting out at a most unnatural angle. It was all too obvious that something serious had happened to the knee-joint. Waves of pain swept over me and my leg felt as if all the demons in hell were waging war on it, armed with a thousand red-hot pokers. The scrum disentangled itself and left me prostrate on the ground. Once it became obvious to them that I would not be able to walk I was picked up by some of my brawny fellow players and carried unceremoniously to the touchline.

In this way, in 1934 at the age of seventeen, my rugby playing career came to an end in the middle of my last season at school. A few months later an operation was performed on the offending limb and thankfully it was successful enough to allow me to walk again without limping. However, the surgeon advised me against making any further incursions into the rugby field. He warned me against ever playing the game again on the threat of a shortened leg, should it be re-injured.

As a bonus he added: 'It should stand up to most things except being pulled.'

I've often thought it has been receiving this treatment unmercifully ever since.

The surgeon's advice saddened me immensely. Since I had been a young boy I had always taken an active interest in sport and during my latter days in school had played both cricket and rugby. The thought of not being able to take part any more brought about my first acute feeling of depression, to be followed a little later by an overwhelming sense of bitterness against the act of fate that had dealt me such a cruel blow.

However, at seventeen the impetuous feelings of youth are but fleeting phases which, once encountered, can be easily resolved when one looks ahead and realizes that the whole of life is in front. When I thought of this as I lay on top of my bed in my room at home I realized that my misfortune was a small one when set alongside the problems and burdens that so many other people were being forced to bear.

I decided to find an alternative way in which to spend my weekends and at first my thoughts centred on joining the local Territorial Army Unit. While examining a directory giving a list of personnel in each of the Glasgow Territorial units my eye alighted on an entry which read: 'No. 602 City of Glasgow Bomber Squadron A.A.F.' Quite frankly until that moment I had never even heard of the Auxiliary Air Force. Nevertheless I considered it worthwhile finding out more. That night I wrote to the adjutant, Flight Lieutenant G. S. Hodson, later to become an Air Vice-Marshal, and several days later received a most courteous reply inviting me to call to see him any weekend at the R.A.F. station at Abbotsinch.

It was a glorious October Saturday afternoon and various types of aircraft were engaged in sundry exercises—Hawker Harts, a Westland Wapiti and a few silver coloured Avro 504's, old-fashioned two-bayed biplanes of World War I vintage. These had been brought up to date by the adoption of a Lynx engine instead of the old rotary Gnome and a modified under-carriage without the familiar skid to prevent the aircraft from tipping up on its nose.

Abbotsinch had only been recently opened as an airfield and apart from a solitary hangar and a few station administrative buildings it consisted otherwise of a large grass field—a far cry indeed from the modern civil airport that it is now, linking Glasgow with London and the Continent.

I was introduced to the Commanding Officer, Squadron Leader the Marquis of Douglas and Clydesdale, who, after asking the expected questions of age, education and so on, asked me if I had ever done any flying.

I stammered as I replied. It seemed incongruous to be asking to join a squadron when one had not done any flying. 'No, sir, I've never been up in an aeroplane.'

His warm smile put me at ease. 'Never mind, there's got to be a first time for everything. Would you like to go up now?'

With these words Lord Clydesdale set me on the path that was to start me as a weekend flier and eventually, due to the circumstances of war, give me a career where no matter what was to happen my over-riding passion would be for flying.

The adjutant had one of the old 504's wheeled out and started up while I donned fleece-lined sheepskin flying boots, leather gauntlets, flying helmet, a Sidcot suit, fur-trimmed flying goggles and a parachute. Due to the bulkiness of this unfamiliar clothing it took several minutes to manœuvre myself into the small and extremely uncomfortable rear cockpit. Hodson climbed into the front, ran up the engine and started to taxi the aircraft to the far side of the aerodrome. There was no inter-communication system between the two cockpits and as we sped over the grass I felt isolated, but somehow exhilarated by the prospect of the flight that lay ahead.

Eventually we took off and I was surprised to find the 504 several feet off the ground and going into a steady climb. I had been sure that take-off would have been much more exciting. There seemed to be very little sensation whatsoever and I thought to myself, 'If it's as easy as all this I shouldn't have much of a job learning to fly!'

As we climbed I was astonished by the amount of water I could see near and around Glasgow. I could distinguish the skeleton hull of 'No. 534'—the name by which the *Queen Mary* was known before she was launched—taking shape in John Brown's shipyard and the point where the Black and White Cart rivers met to become one before flowing into the mighty Clyde. The sight of this vast panorama of small lakes, lochs and reservoirs, together with the new view I was obtaining of many of the more familiar landmarks, excited me more than anything had done in the past. If this was what flying gave you, then I was all for it, I mused.

No sooner had I become accustomed to the smoothness of the climb than Hodson levelled out at what must have been about three thousand feet. After several minutes of level flight I felt the 504 doing a slow roll to starboard. This was followed by a similar manœuvre to port. Naturally, I felt slightly alarmed by these new tactics but above all felt silly, hanging upside down with my feet banging helplessly against the instrument panel. But there was nothing I could do about it except stare forcibly at the hunched shoulders of the pilot in the cockpit ahead of me and will him to stop throwing the aircraft about and settle down to some straightforward flying.

Hodson had warned me, prior to take-off, that I was on no account to put my feet on the rudder bar or my hands on the joystick. I felt great difficulty in obeying his orders as I found myself doing all manner of aerobatics without the slightest knowledge of what was really happening. My first concern was for my wallet and the loose change in my pockets. What would happen if they fell out? I had visions of coins dropping from the skies and causing a minor sensation on the ground beneath me. Shortly afterwards I remarked about this to the late Jimmie Whitelaw, brother of George Whitelaw, the humorous artist, when he asked me for my first impressions of flying.

He passed my views on to his brother who sketched an appropriate picture which was later published in *Punch* under the title of 'The Flying Scotsman'.

My first flight lasted about thirty minutes and for most of it I don't think we were the right way up for more than a quarter of that time, or so it seemed. However, it was intended to be a test of endurance, or so I was told afterwards. The fact that I was able to stow away a large afternoon tea shortly after landing dispelled any fears they may have had about my reactions in the air. I left for home with a promise from George Hodson that I would hear from them in due course, but more than three months passed before I was requested to attend for a medical examination. I got through this and a fortnight later received my first service orders—to report the following weekend for initial training.

The most trivial things stick in my mind about those early days. I shall never forget, for instance, how impressed I was when I saw Marcus Robinson step out of a Hart, having just taxied in after completing his first solo. He was to me, then, a sort of superman who could actually pilot one of these impressive looking aeroplanes. I will always remember, too, the smell of petrol fumes as they came to one in the cockpit of an Avro 504. It was a smell unlike anything else—distinctive, like the aroma of fumes you associate with the traffic-laden London streets. I well remember too that awful feeling of frustration in having to sit in the crew room reading Standing Orders when I would have given anything to be out and about getting on with my initial instruction in the air. I still sometimes laugh to myself when I think of how every time the door opened both my friend, John Hawkes, and I would jump eagerly to our feet hoping that it was Hodson or Mark Selway, the assistant adjutant, to tell us that we might go for 'a trip around the sky'.

When the proper business of flying did eventually get under way it was at a slow and leisurely pace. In the first four months of 1935 I only succeeded in logging a little over seven hours' air time. Rate-one turns to the left, rate-one turns to the right, gliding turns, 'S' approaches—these were the order of the day.

All the same the training was thorough despite the snail-like pace and gradually, bit by bit, the intricacies of aviating unravelled themselves until the long-awaited climax to every would-be pilot's course came along. The day of the first solo.

It was a calm, clear Thursday evening in April—an ideal time to be flying with the atmosphere crystal clear and no turbulence to rattle the quiet serenity of the occasion.

Hodson, sitting in the front seat of the 504, had guided me round the circuit for three trial 'circuits and bumps' and I soon discovered that when we took off, climbed to one thousand feet and came round on a rate-one turn, we always passed over the same small farmhouse with its mottled blue tiled roof. I also found out that, if I closed the throttle at one thousand feet just as I came swooping in over the railway line which ran near to the aerodrome boundary, and started to turn in towards the field when over the third railway signal from the Paisley end, we made a first-class approach and landed easily. I was pleased with my performance and Hodson, occupying the front cockpit, seemed to have no cause for complaint. After landing for the third time it took me completely by surprise when my instructor suddenly turned round and shouted.

His words were lost above the noise of the engine.

'What's that?' I bellowed.

He waved his hand at me and turning again brought the 504 to a halt. The engine ticked over with a strong and regular beat. Hodson turned round once more. 'That was fine,' he said, 'now you can go up and have a go by yourself.'

The tranquillity of the evening, the thrill of moving through the sky and of being able to look down from my small eyrie on the ever-changing landscape—all these were shattered for me when I heard his remarks. For me the peace was smashed and a thousand possible dangers seemed to loom up out of the atmosphere ready to grasp at the unsuspecting novice.

Hodson was giving me no opportunities to have second thoughts. Almost as soon as he had finished speaking he was climbing out of his cockpit. I sat watching him as he tied up all the loose safety harness straps so that they should not foul the dual controls in the front seat. I could feel my heart pounding and my mouth growing dry as the moment of truth approached at what, for me, was an alarming speed. Then, to my amazement, he produced three or four long multi-coloured streamers which he proceeded to tie to the outside struts of the wings.

He was swift to answer my question explaining that they were there to warn all other aircraft in the vicinity that here was a poor soul dicing with death for the very first time. Later on, training aircraft were to be painted yellow and the use of streamers abandoned. The attachment of the streamers took some time and with every extra minute the nervousness and tension increased. At last he was finished. He jumped up on the wing and shouted his last-minute instructions, at the same time checking my cockpit to see that everything was wound the way it ought to be wound.

'Just do the same as you have been doing these last few circuits,' he said, 'and I'll wait here until you land. Then you can pick me up and taxi me to the hangar.'

With a sickly smile I nodded assent, having long since lost all semblance of a voice, my throat was so dry. He gave me a quick thumbs-up sign then was gone from the wing. I was alone —the moment I had waited for with eager anticipation was now really upon me. The controls—the switches and buttons— which I had been trained to use until they were as familiar to me as the fingers on my hands took on the appearance of lethal weapons. I looked out from my lonely seat and saw Hodson watching from a short distance away. I decided to get something done fairly quickly before my hesitance drew his attention. Slowly, I opened the throttle and the old 504 wobbled and trundled its way across the aerodrome. As we moved, my pilot's instincts—what little I had at that time—gradually started to take hold of me, suppressing the fears and the doubts.

Without realizing it I found the procedure for take-off running through my mind. 'Head into the slight breeze, open the throttle gently, get the tail up and hold it straight on the rudder as soon as the speed begins to build up, 50 m.p.h. on the clock and a gentle pressure on the stick . . .'

I was airborne and the faithful Avro was behaving herself remarkably well as she took me up, up and away from the aerodrome. I let out a shout of joy; I was aloft, no one had helped me; at last I was master of my own aircraft—or so I thought.

As I went upwards I sensed that the climb seemed to be at an abnormal rate. Only then did it dawn on me that, of course, the aircraft would take off with a much shorter run, having only one body to carry instead of the accustomed two. The result was that I was well over 1500 feet when I levelled off and on my way round the circuit this was increased to a little over two thousand feet. All my carefully laid plans for shutting off the engine at the third railway signal had now to be abandoned and a hastily conceived plan put into operation.

Looking over the side of the aircraft I could just see the tiny, forlorn figure of Hodson standing patiently at the far side of the aerodrome waiting to be picked up and taxied in to the hangar. That was my main concern, despite my other difficulties —I must pick up Hodson and taxi him to the hangar.

Now we were coming up on the railway line again. What should I do? Perhaps I'd better go a bit further over this time as I'm a bit higher up, I thought. Yes, that was the plan, I decided. So over I went, waited until I was opposite my friendly third signal from the Paisley end, closed the throttle and turned in towards the aerodrome. My aiming point by this time had become the unfortunate Hodson, still patiently waiting for his lift to the hangar and looking upwards, no doubt wondering what his scatter-brained pupil was getting up to.

I was certain that the Avro was moving too fast for a normal glide in to land but couldn't be sure whether or not my imagination was playing tricks on me. However, I was still pointing at Hodson who was increasing in size as I got nearer. Over the boundary I went, urging the 504 onwards and down. The air-speed indicator showed 105 m.p.h. When I was about thirty yards short of him I decided this was the moment to get on to the earth. I levelled off, bounced hard on the ground with such force that the trusty old aircraft seemed to tremble, then to my utter amazement I was in the air again and sailing past my unfortunate instructor. I'll never forget the fleeting glimpse I had of the tortured expression on his face as I swept past. It was the expression of a man who would never forgive; the look of a man who has been betrayed.

But the red face was gone in an instant. I forgot about him while I tried to get down once more. Thump—the wheels were on the ground again. Then there was nothing—just a feeling of weightlessness. Heaven forbid, I thought, I'm going up again. Sure enough the determined World War I veteran was not going to be landed by such a clumsy, heavy-handed individual as myself. Take to the air, it's much safer, seemed to be her motto. I forced her back again on the grass. Thump—the fuselage shook; the engine roared its annoyance. The shattering effect of this latest touchdown made me realize that I seemed to be going a little faster than was intended for an Avro 504 to land gracefully.

As the thought rushed through my mind the 504 was in the air again—this time no more than three feet up. Thump—she connected with Mother Earth yet again. Then she was flying again. By this time the big hangar was looming large and solid in front of me. There would soon be little grass left for my pantomime act. Thump . . . thump . . . thump . . . thump—first the wheels, then the tail skid alternately making contact with the ground as the old Avro continued to bucket across the field like some monstrous old hen.

Finally the aircraft stopped attempting to return to the skies she knew so well. I succeeded in cutting back the speed and after a jarring crunch was able to bring her to a standstill almost in front of the hangar. The sweat pouring from me, I switched off and climbed out. Jumping on to the grass I held on to the wing and looked around me. There was no sign of life from the hangar. I was not surprised. Anyone who might have been showing a mild interest in what was going on had long since fled for shelter as they witnessed my unorthodox approach.

Away in the distance I could see the small figure of Hodson, his parachute slung over his shoulder, trudging wearily across the grass. At this point my elation at landing safely, no matter how badly, left me as I thought of the torrent of abuse which would surely be showered on me when my instructor arrived. I had already heard him on one of the rare occasions when his temper had been roused, and the outburst could certainly make stronger men than me quail.

I never did find out whether the long walk back had exhausted him or whether the time he took to get back was sufficiently long for his temper to cool down or whether he was just downright relieved to see the aircraft and me both still in one piece. Fifteen minutes later he reached me, red-faced and perspiring from the exertion of walking such a distance in heavy flying clothing, plus the added weight of his parachute. For a moment he didn't speak; he just stared long and hard in my direction.

'Not bad,' he said when he had recovered his breath. He came up and put his hand on my shoulder. 'Not bad, Sandy. However, that'll do for tonight. Now for drinks all round—on you.'

Too relieved to say anything I only ventured a quick smile and set off with him in the direction of the crew room. A few feet from the door he stopped and looked at me.

'Oh by the way, Sandy, there's one thing you must remember in future. A landing should always be the successful conclusion of a flight—not the bloody end of everything.'

The first solo stage being passed it then became a matter of time, patience and a constant battle against that dreaded enemy of all trainee pilots—over-confidence—before I was commissioned as a Pilot Officer in the Auxiliary Air Force. In July, while we were carrying out our annual training at North Coates Fittes in Lincolnshire, I started flying the Hawker Hart. I had only one experience of Harts before this—and as a passenger. During the previous February a combined rugby team comprised of members of the two Scottish Auxiliary Squadrons, 602 and 603 (City of Edinburgh) set off by air for Usworth, near Newcastle, to play an English Auxiliary Squadrons XV. Five Harts from Glasgow and the same number from Edinburgh were involved. It was the first time I had been up in a Hart and I was flying as passenger with Flight Lieutenant Douglas Farquhar, 'C' Flight Commander. For that matter I was being foolhardy enough to ignore my doctor's advice about not playing any more rugger.

All went well as we flew eastwards from Abbotsinch to Turnhouse, near Edinburgh, where we circled while 603 Squadron's Flight took off. Turning southwards we crossed the Border, about twenty-five miles west of Berwick-on-Tweed. Almost immediately it started to snow. The weather forecast we had received prior to departure had not given us any indication of this and so Douglas Farquhar, who was leading the formation, decided to press on in the hope that it was only a passing snow shower.

The white flakes swirled in dense clouds and as the minutes passed the storm increased until in next to no time we were being buffeted about in the face of a severe gale which was whipping the snow into a blizzard. At this time there were no highly developed wireless navigational aids to assist the unwary pilot as there are nowadays. It was a case of the individual being left to work out his own salvation as best he could.

Douglas, with Jimmie Hodge and Andrew Rintoul, both pilots of considerable experience, tucked in beside his Hart, swung the formation eastwards to strike the coast. The two outside aircraft were being flown by comparatively junior pilots, Marcus Robinson and John Shewell.

We hit the coast just south of Alnwick and it was decided to try to return to Turnhouse rather than attempt to find Usworth which was difficult enough to locate even in the best of circumstances. Douglas manœuvred his formation northwards and we crept on along the coast as the snow became thicker and thicker. By the time we reached the River Forth our petrol supply was becoming low and the visibility was such that it was humanly impossible to make more than a very rough guess at one's position. Having only, by the skin of our teeth, avoided colliding with the Forth Railway Bridge, as luck had it encountering it between two of the three enormous cantilevers instead of, as might well have been the case, directly opposite one of them, Douglas gave the signal to break formation. It was every man for himself.

Douglas turned his aircraft eastwards again to try to pick up the Forth Bridge once more but must have passed it without seeing it. I certainly saw no sign of the giant construction due to the density of the storm. Shortly afterwards as we were creeping along the coast at a height of about fifty feet and almost one hundred yards offshore the engine came to an abrupt stop. The fuel had run out.

Swinging the Hart towards the shore Douglas shouted to me

at the top of his voice to hang on. I needed no bidding. Now that the engine had stopped running the silence seemed to make our situation even more precarious. The snow swirling and eddying, and only clearing sufficiently to give us occasional glimpses of the shore, had assumed ghostly proportions.

Through a gap in the storm Douglas saw the sand and skilfully brought the Hart downwind to land. We were lucky— it was the only stretch of sand around for miles—it was Porto- bello beach. The sturdy Hart bounced along the uneven terrain and lurched over a couple of sewage pipes before coming to a jerky halt near the water's edge.

Glumly, we climbed out and surveyed the scene. The only occupant of the promenade appeared to be an old man who was out exercising his dog. Why he should have ventured out on such a mission during a severe storm beats me, but he clambered down on to the beach, followed by his faithful pet, and asked if he could be of any assistance. By the time we had exchanged a few pleasantries dozens of willing helpers had appeared on the scene.

As the tide was rising quickly we had the aircraft man- handled along the beach to a slipway and pushed up on to the road. There we tethered one wing to a lamp-post and the other to a drinking fountain. Having asked a policeman to stand guard, Douglas and I set off to find out what had become of the rest of the party.

We boarded a tramcar and made for the nearest police station. On the way we passed Hodge's aircraft sitting up on its nose in a ploughed field by the roadside, looking for all the world like some gigantic totem pole. At the next stop we dashed off the tram without paying our fares and ran back to see if we could find Hodge. As we made our way across the upturned furrows I caught sight of him standing sheltering from the wind beside his aircraft, a pained expression on his face. He was quick to tell us the reason for this. Jimmie Hodge was a small man and when he finally came to rest with his aircraft's tail high in the air he found that his cockpit was a long way from the ground. Too far to jump, so he decided that his only means of exit was forward over the engine cowling. Climbing out, he slithered down only to find that the cowling was still extremely hot. Fortunately, his feelings were more inflamed than his person.

After a bit of searching we discovered that Shewell had been less fortunate. His aircraft had turned on its back, but without injury to himself. Rintoul and Robinson were more fortunate, having pulled off good forced landings. The Edinburgh fellows did not fare much better than ourselves, although only one of their aircraft came to grief. This was an unfortunate case as the pilot, not being able to distinguish grass and ploughed land, owing to the amount of snow on the ground, decided to land on a long straight stretch of road. He did this and set his Hart down in a text book landing. The aircraft raced merrily along and all was going well until he came to a corner.

There were no brakes on the Harts so he had no option but to go straight on. This resulted in his somersaulting over a ditch and a hedge before he finally came to rest upside down in a neighbouring field. His injuries were only superficial ones.

It was a dejected and dispirited bunch of airmen who gathered together later in the day to try to sort out all the problems concerned with the recovery of the various abandoned aircraft. Nevertheless the main reason for our dejection was that we had missed what had promised to be a first-rate game of rugby.

Apart from putting in an appearance at Abbotsinch practically every Saturday afternoon and all day on Sundays we had to attend regularly at our town headquarters in Glasgow for periods of drill, and lectures on navigation, bombing, gunnery and a variety of subjects.

We had with us an extremely intelligent and delightful individual, Brian Smith, who was employed in the design office of Barr and Stroud's optical and precision instrument factory at Anniesland, near Glasgow.

During one of our evening lectures, given by a corporal armourer, on the latest mark of bombsight, our instructor was laboriously explaining its method of operation to us.

'And now, gentlemen, you align this sight fore and aft and, by manipulating this little screw here, you bring the pointer of the wind scale to read zero.'

'I don't think so, corporal,' said a loud voice from the back of the room.

'Excuse me, sir' . . . the corporal waved one hand to silence the interrupter . . . 'as I was saying, gentlemen, you align the sight fore and aft and, by manipulating this little screw here, you bring the pointer of the wind scale to read zero.'

'I'm sorry, corporal, I don't think you're correct,' said the same voice once more.

The corporal looked furious. Glaring at the back of the room he said, quite firmly: 'Sir—I am giving this lecture, but before we go any further, would you kindly inform me why you are so certain that I'm wrong?'

'By all means,' said Brian, getting to his feet. 'You see, I happened to design the damned thing.'

The audience convulsed in laughter and the poor corporal looked extremely shamefaced. However, the lecture went on— given this time by Brian, with the corporal as an interested listener.

3 Night flight extraordinary

In 1936 the first of the R.A.F. regular squadrons to be posted to Abbotsinch arrived for a short stay. Their visit was brief and short lived: they were blown away during a freak gale which at times reached well over 100 m.p.h. Unfortunately the only permanently built hangar on the aerodrome was occupied by 602 squadron and the regular squadron had to make do with four or five of the temporary Bessoneaux type. They were indeed temporary shelters.

One of the hangars actually became airborne in the height of the gale and travelled about one hundred and fifty yards before coming to rest on top of the Sergeants' Mess. Fortunately, no one was injured, but the squadron lost practically all of its aircraft and eventually had to be re-equipped and re-formed elsewhere. From then on, however, we always had another squadron at Abbotsinch with us, not that we saw a great deal of them as they were generally off-duty during the periods when we were operating.

One of the highlights of our annual training used to come when a flight of a regular fighter squadron was stationed with us for two weeks to carry out what were called affiliation exercises. There was one occasion when a highly amusing and most unusual incident occurred which caused a few red faces.

Three Hinds, with which we had been re-equipped, of 'B' Flight took off to do an affiliation exercise with a flight of Hawker Furies of No. 1 Squadron. George Pinkerton was the pilot of one of the aircraft with L.A.C. Train as his rear-gunner. When the formation was up at fifteen thousand feet George felt his controls becoming very stiff to operate and guessed that Train had accidentally stood on one of the control wires which led through to the rear cockpit.

This, in fact, was exactly what had happened, as the rear-gunner was hopping about all over the cockpit in an effort to get good camera gun shots of the attacking fighters.

Not having any vocal intercommunication system George turned round to Train and with violent gesticulations made signs to him to take his 'ruddy great feet' off the control wires. Train stared at the frantic looking pilot for several seconds, then completely misunderstanding George's signals and thinking that the aircraft was completely out of control donned his parachute pack and leaped smartly over the side. All George could do was watch with an amazed look as Train got his parachute sorted out. His shouts were carried away on the wind and lost above the roar of the engine and the more he shouted and waved his hands the more alarmed became the rear-gunner.

When Train baled out the formation was over Aberfoyle and a strong west wind was blowing. By the time he descended his fifteen thousand feet he did not touch earth again until near Kippen, almost thirty miles away. As he vanished from sight George flew on, the controls of the Hind now operating perfectly.

It was in the middle of June, 1936, when Group Captain David MacIntyre asked me to join him at a Flying School he intended to open. We were standing beside our Avro Tutor aircraft in a field bordering the road which ran between Monkton and Adamton, two small villages situated a few miles north of Prestwick, in Ayrshire, when he made his suggestion.

'How about it, Sandy?' he asked. 'We hope to have the airfield and the Flying School opened before the end of the year. I'd like you to come and join us.'

'I wish I could, Mac,' I replied 'But I can't very well walk out on my present job and, besides, I haven't got my instructor's category.'

'Too bad,' said Mac. 'Never mind though—maybe later.' The conversation over, we climbed back into the Tutor and took off again to return to our base at Abbotsinch. Little did I realize at the time that this was an historic moment; for that was the first time an aircraft had landed on that spot—which in the course of the next decade was to become one of the most used and best known airfields in the world—Prestwick Airport.

David MacIntyre and Lord Clydesdale, the former succeeding the latter as Commanding Officer of 602 Squadron just about this time, had recently inaugurated a company to provide one of many Civilian Flying Training Schools then being formed throughout the country to boost up training for the Royal Air Force—the Government having realized, rather belatedly, that the R.A.F. was woefully under strength and that only a crash programme of this sort could hope to turn out the numbers of new pilots which were urgently needed. There were many indications that Hitler and his Nazi followers were making military preparations far in excess of those required for the internal security of Germany alone.

Both Lord Clydesdale and MacIntyre had already done much to put Scotland on the aviation map by being the first, and until then the only, people to have conquered Mount Everest when they piloted the two Westland Wallace aircraft of the successful Houston-Everest Expedition in 1933. Mac, who so tragically lost his life in a flying accident in North Africa in 1958, was the true founder and chief dynamo of that great Scottish enterprise —Scottish Aviation Limited.

At the time, I was working with a footwear firm in Edinburgh, but I had already come to the conclusion that I was not really cut out for that sort of life! I lived for the weekends when I could travel through to Paisley to get on with my flying. Therefore, Mac's casual remark continued to course through my mind but I couldn't see how I was ever going to be able to get the necessary courses to become a flying instructor.

However, early in 1938 Scottish Aviation Limited extended its scope when No. 1 Civil Air Navigation School was opened up at Prestwick to augment the training of navigators and keep pace with the increased output of pilots.

I wasted no time in contacting MacIntyre to see whether he

could find me a niche in his new enterprise. To my unbounded joy, he agreed to take me on in a supernumerary capacity until I was able to gain the required civilian flying licences—a pilot 'B' licence and a civil navigator's licence.

I can't say that it exactly broke my heart when I severed my connections with the shoe trade and I was very happy indeed to install myself in the staff mess at Prestwick alongside those other stalwarts, John Dobson, Douglas Shields, George Reid, Bill Jennens, 'Cap' Capper and Irvine Chalmers-Watson. Straight away I was given plenty of flying to do of a non-instructional nature and was able to help out with a number of ground lectures. At the same time, I set about qualifying myself to sit for the necessary licences.

I had already amassed sufficient hours in my pilot's log book to satisfy the examiners on that score. However, before I could be issued with the 'B' licence, I also had to satisfy them that I was proficient on instrument flying and that I was capable of flying a cross-country route in the dark. For a variety of reasons, the test for the latter turned out to be somewhat erratic.

In July, 1938, I took the opportunity to do some flying with the Cinque Ports Flying Club while attending the annual training period with 602 Squadron at Hawkinge, near Folkestone. The little clubhouse at Lympne was a focal point for all private flying enthusiasts and it didn't matter two hoots whether you were Jim Mollison, Geoffrey de Havilland, Amy Johnson or just plain uninteresting Flying Officer Johnstone. Whoever you were, a warm welcome was guaranteed from the club members.

In the course of having a drink in the bar with the Chief Flying Instructor, David Llewellyn, I told him about my efforts to gain my 'B' licence and how, at the moment, all I was short of was the night flying test.

'Get yourself made a temporary member here, old boy, and I'll give you one of our kites to use!'

I took his advice and joined the club and soon after made an application to carry out the necessary cross-country flight whenever conditions were right for the test. This meant waiting until there was a period of no moon; but the route to be flown was standard—a flight at not less than 2,000 feet from Croydon to Lympne on a full-black night.

Arrangements were made for the test to be scrutinized at both ends and I duly turned up that morning to collect a suitable aeroplane from David.

'Sorry we're a bit short of decent crates, Sandy, but I think we have one that should just about get you there and back!'

I had my doubts about the veracity of this statement when I saw what was being offered. A really aged Gypsy I Moth was being wheeled out of the hangar, dark red in colour, with one of those inverted engines on it which successfully obscured the pilot's forward vision. It was not done to wear a parachute when flying in a club machine, presumably to discourage too many panicky aviators from abandoning their aircraft at the first sign of trouble. Therefore the pilot's seating position in the cockpit was much lower than I had previously been used to when flying in Service aircraft. Indeed, when I climbed in and sat down, I must have looked from the outside like some terrified doomie sitting there with only my nose peeping over the cockpit combing.

With certain qualms, but very grateful for the loan, I flew the old Moth to Croydon in daylight to position it ready for the flight back to Lympne that night. The required full-black conditions were not due until after 11.30 p.m. and so, arranging with the airport authorities to have the scrutineer and ground crew available at the appropriate time, I pushed off into town to have a meal and to visit a local cinema.

To my horror, conditions were decidedly foggy when I left the picture-house and made my way back to Croydon. The controller on duty in the Flying Control tower said he thought the fog was only local but he would telephone through to Lympne and ask them what the weather was doing over there. The reply was reassuring so I arranged a take-off time and went downstairs to meet the official who was acting as the scrutineer and found him standing beside my little aircraft with an ordinary household barograph tucked under his arm.

'Where would you like me to put this?' he asked as I approached.

'What do you mean?' I replied, puzzled as to why he should want me to act as a courier for this mundane little piece of household weather gadgetry.

'Well, you've got to take this thing with you, you know! It's a sealed barograph which I have set to zero and which will confirm that you have kept above the required two thousand feet during your flight.'

So bang went my hopes of sneaking my way up the main roads towards Dover, which I reckoned I would be able to follow easily by the headlights of the motor traffic that, even in 1938, was prolific in these parts.

'This obviously isn't my day!' I thought to myself as I watched the wretched instrument being secured away in the little locker just aft of the rear cockpit. 'Oh well, I will just have to do it the hard way, after all.'

Having strapped myself into the cockpit, I could barely distinguish the blurred features of the ground mechanic who was standing by the prop, ready to swing the engine into life.

'Switches off, petrol on—suck on!'

I repeated the instructions back to him when he turned the propeller by hand a few times to build up a little compression in the cylinders. Once again he stood to one side, his hand resting on the topmost tip of the propeller.

'Switches on—contact!'

With a cough and a splutter, the Gypsy engine fired into life and I was now committed. Checking that my navigation lights were burning correctly, I waved away the chocks and trundled out towards the take-off point close by the large chance light which served to illuminate the flarepath. From there, it all looked alarmingly dark and foggy ahead.

As my aeroplane was not fitted with any form of wireless, I waited until the flarepath controller shone a green light towards me, which was the signal that all was clear for me to go ahead.

I opened the throttle and bumped off into the blackness ahead. We were airborne in next to no time and I soon found myself flying over the southern outskirts of London.

The sight of those myriads of street lights, interspersed with a large number of neon signs, was so breathtaking that for a moment or so I was too fascinated to do anything else but admire the scene. However, the thought of the tell-tale barograph locked up behind me soon brought me back to reality while I climbed up over the airfield to reach the necessary height before setting course for Lympne.

As soon as I cleared the outskirts of London it became apparent that the worst of my fears were groundless and that the weather ahead was indeed as clear as a bell. In the middle distance I could easily make out the first of the Air Navigation beacons at Methersden which had been set up to assist certain airlines to track more easily in and out of Croydon.

Further away I could pick out the second of these, at Beryle, and it was not long before the flashing beacon on the roof of the hangar at Lympne rose into view flashing its red 'de-dah', 'de-dah', the morse letter 'A'.

However, owing to my forward vision being obscured by the upside-down engine in the Moth, I had to turn the aircraft to one side or the other to see what lay dead ahead, and every time I did this the nose appeared to drop alarmingly. I later found that the 'cheese cutter' or tail trimming device, tended to slip and this was what was throwing my aircraft out of proper flying trim.

To add to my discomfort, the long exhaust pipe which ran back from the engine, close by the cockpit combing, had become red hot and this put my nose in considerable jeopardy every time I looked out to port.

In this way, I progressed towards the east in a series of jerky turns to the left, each one accompanied by an alarming lurch earthwards, and eventually arrived over Lympne where I prepared to let down in to the small flarepath of goose-neck flares, which had been lit to await my arrival.

Fortunately a chance light was also in position at this end of the trip for, just as I was rounding out and coming in over the hedge, a small crowd of people spread right across my path, gesticulating wildly, all waving some glistening objects in their hands.

I immediately opened up to go round again, wondering as I

did so what in the name of Goodwin could be wrong. Had I lost part of my undercarriage, or was something else hanging loose of which I was unaware?

I tried a turn to the left, then another to the right; I pulled the stick back and made the aeroplane climb; I put negative 'G' on by pushing the stick forward, but could discern nothing out of the ordinary with the old Moth. So, making a final pass at low level up the flarepath to make sure that it was by now clear of people, I turned sharply to port, touched down and bounced into the blackness beyond the welcome ray of the chance light.

As soon as the aircraft came to rest, half a dozen pairs of hands reached down into the cockpit and dragged me out of it. I was carried, shoulder high, to the clubhouse where a thundering good party seemed to be taking place. The crowd on the flarepath had, in fact, only been some of the revellers, glasses in hand, bent on greeting me, as if I were a world record breaker completing an epic flight. They obviously thought little of my prowess as an aviator and had not reckoned that I would get in first time anyway.

After getting rid of my flying kit and downing a very welcome half pint, I joined Llewellyn, who had been appointed scrutineer at the Lympne end of the flight, and went round to the hangar into which the Moth had by now been pushed. Unlocking the barograph he took off the cylindrical roll of paper and held it under the light.

'Crikey!' was all he said.

On it was a tracing which would have done credit to a schoolboy's efforts to draw a squeezed-up plan view of the Alps. However, I was very much relieved to see that the tell-tale line, with all its zigs up and its zags down, never came below the two thousand feet mark during the requisite period of the flight. It apparently satisfied my examiners as I obtained my commercial pilot's licence soon afterwards.

Next, I had to turn my attention to the navigator's licence, but I was greatly helped in this by getting posted on to a Service navigation course at Manston under the aegis of 602 Squadron. This provided me with the necessary qualification except for three subjects, International Air Legislation, Signals and Meteorology but, having received sufficient coaching on all three to enable me to pass the written papers, I set off to the Ministry of Civil Aviation in the Strand to take the final, and practical, part of the examinations.

Having apparently succeeded in convincing the signals experts that I could read and send morse and semaphore to the required standard and the legal experts that I knew what it meant when I saw an airship drifting by with two black balls hanging below it, I repaired to the Kingsway Headquarters of the Meteorological Service for my ultimate test.

In this instance my examiner was an elderly gentleman, pedantic in manner and clipped of speech.

'Trace me the course of these frontal systems you see illustrated on that synoptic chart,' he began, handing me a large meteorological chart well covered with isobars squeezed into a number of identifiable patterns. From this, we progressed to other more complex details affecting the study of weather until he finally turned to me and said, 'Young man, what do you know about thunderstorms?'

Well, here was something which I had studied a good deal, for I was fascinated by the theory of how they formed; the drops of moisture being whirled up in the strong up-currents of air ever increasing in size until they became unstable, when they would break up into tiny droplets, creating a small electrical charge as they did so, and so on until a full-scale thundercloud developed and the inevitable big spark jumped from one end of the cloud to the other, or from one cloud to another. I described all this in much detail and I was able to reel it off pat while my examiner sat, smugly I thought, listening to this masterly exposition. I should have stopped there but, no—I was determined to let him hear how well I had studied the subject. I added at the end: 'Well, that's the so-called Simpson's theory of thunderstorms, but I'm told that it's really nothing but a lot of twaddle. However, I haven't been able to lay my hands on the up-to-date theory but I'll try to get the true story as soon as possible.'

'Well, it's good enough to be going on with. You'll do!' answered my examiner curtly.

I thanked him and left the room. As I shut the door, my eye happened to catch sight of the occupant's name-card pinned to it—Doctor Simpson, Director. What else could I do but take to my heels?

4 *Death claims a friend*

On returning to Prestwick, complete with a brand new 'B' licence, I got down to the serious business of trying to turn out navigators in ten weeks from fellows who had just come in from civilian life. It was a hard, enjoyable job, lecturing and flying alternately, but in the end the results were passably good and I think our pupils left with, at least, a thorough basic grounding in the mysterious art of air navigation.

I was also gaining considerable flying experience myself as a member of 602 Squadron. Avro 504's, Avro Tutors, Harts, Hinds, Battles, Wellesleys, Tiger Moths, Hectors, Gloster Gauntlets and various other types of aircraft had made their mark in my pilot's log book. In my capacity as an instructor at Prestwick, I was also piling up a fair number of hours on Avro Ansons.

My fellow instructors were few in number. Apart from John Dobson, who remained with Scottish Aviation Ltd. for many years, there was George Reid, a Canadian by birth, who was to die tragically while commanding a Beaufighter squadron in North Africa, Bill Jennens, an ex-Imperial Airways pilot, Douglas Shields, who like Reid and myself was still in the Auxiliary Air Force, Bunny Vetch, an ex-R.A.F. pilot who was also to lose his life during the war, 'Sausage' Palethorpe, an ex-R.A.F. sergeant pilot, and 'Farmer' Giles, another ex-Imperial Airways type.

My friendship with Douglas began shortly after I was accepted for training with 602 Squadron. Douglas, who was a member of 603 Squadron at Turnhouse, was one of those men who always seem to have a happy expression on their faces. He was also a hard worker and full of resolve and courage. It was both good fun and a rewarding experience to work alongside him at Prestwick.

We were flying Ansons at the time and it was our normal custom to carry a safety pilot when undertaking night exercises with our students. We reckoned it was asking too much to leave it all to a single pilot to fly the courses given to him by his pupils and to keep an accurate plot of the aircraft's position in the dark irrespective of whether the courses worked out were right or wrong. During the day it didn't matter so much but, when the weather was bad, or on dark nights, two of us normally went up in each aircraft, the second instructor acting as a safety monitor. The normal complement of our training Ansons consisted of an instructor, who piloted the aircraft, a W/T operator to maintain a wireless link with the ground (our aircraft were not fitted with voice radio) and two student navigators.

The night of January 9, 1939, was black and unfriendly and I had been detailed to act as 'Flarepath Pete' during the first training detail. After this I was to be relieved by Bunny Vetch who, it was reckoned, would have had sufficient time to fly his first sortie in order to take over from me in manning the flarepath. I was then to fly with Douglas as his safety man on the second detail.

Warmly wrapped up in my flying kit I stood in the shelter of a throbbing generator to shield myself against the biting January wind. As I huddled even closer to the source of the heat I spotted the navigation lights of an Anson taxi-ing towards me from the direction of the tarmac. Instead of lining up on the flarepath the aircraft taxied beyond it and lined up close to where I was standing. I saw a familiar figure get out and stroll over towards me. It was Douglas.

He shouted above the whistling of the wind, 'Any sign of Bunny coming in yet?'

I shook my head. 'No, not yet, I'm afraid. Look, don't wait for me if you want to get on.'

Douglas fumbled in the pockets of his flying suit. 'Have you a spare cigarette, Sandy?'

I gave him one and lit up myself. Douglas leaned on the generator. 'I'll wait for five minutes and see if he turns up. O.K.?'

I nodded. For the next few minutes we stood together smoking and discussing the progress—rapid or otherwise—being made by our respective pupils. Even after Douglas had ground out the butt of his cigarette there was still no sign of Bunny's Anson returning. He looked at his wrist-watch.

'Look, Sandy, I think I'd better just carry on. Otherwise we'll never get the hangar doors closed tonight.'

He started to walk away. As he quickened his pace to get back to the warmth of his aircraft and out of the wind, he turned and shouted over his shoulder, 'See you at supper.'

Then he was just a figure scrambling into the aircraft. Without wasting any more time his Anson rolled down the flarepath and took off into the darkness.

We never did get the hangar doors closed that night. Neither did I see Douglas at supper. All through the night we waited, watching and listening for some sight or sound of the Anson, now long overdue. Telephone calls were made to various county police headquarters in Southern Scotland. All failed to bring any comforting news. Almost as soon as the first rays of dawn began to appear in a watery sky every available aircraft and pilot at Prestwick was mustered to carry out a thorough aerial search of the area in which we last knew Douglas had been flying.

Ansons, Tiger Moths and an old scarred Hawker Hart took to the air and spread out to their allotted search areas. At the end of a morning's flying all returned to report negative sightings. While the aircraft were being refuelled we sat around in the crew room sipping coffee and talking of the mystery. It was almost time to get back to the search again when the telephone call we had dreaded came through. The wreckage of an aircraft had been found by a shepherd, burned out and strewn across a high spur on the treacherous Rhinns of Kell in Kirkcudbrightshire. The four occupants were dead.

There was little doubt that this was Douglas and his crew. I felt sick in my heart as I thought back to the previous night and pictured his cheery wave before he took off. The death of my friends was to hit me on several occasions in the future but this, the very first blow, was something that affected me very deeply.

Pete Barrow and a photographer were despatched in a Tiger Moth to confirm the location and bring back pictures of the scene. By the time darkness fell they, too, had failed to return. One disaster had been bad enough but at the thought of a second an air of gloom and deep depression fell on my fellow squadron members. Even when forty-three of us, tired out and bleary-eyed after our all-night vigil and subsequent flights on the fruitless search, set out in a convoy of lorries the thought of having something positive to do did little to lift the gloom.

The disaster had occurred in one of the most inaccessible parts of this Kirkcudbrightshire mountain range and the nearest track along which our vehicles, accompanied by an ambulance, could go, stopped some five miles away. By now the wind, which had been little more than a quiet breeze at Prestwick, was whipping itself into a gale as the currents swirled and eddied among the rocks and crags of the mountainside.

In 1939 there were no R.A.F. mountain rescue teams to call on for assistance. Therefore, it was a makeshift assembly of assorted individuals, some of whom had never been on a mountain in their lives before this, who set off up a boulder-strewn gully in the general direction of where Douglas's aircraft had crashed. Everybody wore flying kit, consisting of heavy sidcot suits and fur-lined boots. Some had leather flying helmets on their heads while others favoured the woollen balaclava variety. To light the way we had a collection of torches and oil hurricane lamps. Most men had a knapsack on their back—packed with sandwiches and pies and something to drink. I was one of the more fortunate. Prior to leaving Prestwick I had slipped a bottle of whisky inside my suit.

Taking it in turns to carry four rolled-up stretchers, this Fred Karno's army plodded behind the local shepherd who had first given warning of the finding of the wreckage. Before very long our party started to spread out as we stumbled and scrambled through the coarse grass and over the rocks of that forbidding mountain. The higher we climbed the colder it became and the wind increased in ferocity.

Soon I found that my breath was freezing and icicles were forming on the lower rim of my helmet as we reached the foot of a steep and solidly frozen slope. Step by step we hacked a foothold in the rock-hard surface. As I looked back I could see tiny specks of light showing where the stragglers had fallen behind the main party. I was almost at the top of this difficult slope and ready to step on to easier ground when I felt my foothold break away beneath me.

As my feet fell away I slipped round and fell face forwards. In this position I bumped and slithered over the ice and stones, the hurricane lamp bouncing along in front. Pies from my knapsack shot over my head as did a couple of packets of sandwiches. Somehow or other I managed to catch hold of a protruding rock and brought my headlong descent to a halt. For a minute I lay gasping, my whole body aching with the beating it had taken. As I ran my hand over my suit I forgot my troubles when I found that my bottle of whisky was still intact.

It took me nearly thirty minutes to regain the ground I had lost and I was utterly exhausted when I made it to the top again. My nearest companion, George Reid, suggested that we both have a breather and we settled down in the lee of a large boulder to eat some food and enjoy a dram from the charmed bottle. When we set off again we had not gone far before George shouted to me.

'Come here, Sandy. Have a look at this. It must be jolly steep over here.' I could see the powerful beam of his torch fading away into the blackness. When I joined him I tried to follow the beam of light as he swung it from side to side. We seemed to be standing on the edge of a giant chasm, but we couldn't be certain. Try as we might we could not make up our minds what it was we were facing.

George made the decision. 'Let's get to hell out of here. I think we'd better go back and try to find the track.'

Thank goodness we did. When we repassed this spot in daylight almost twelve hours later we were both horrified to find that we had been standing on the edge of a sheer drop of almost four hundred feet.

We found the rough track again and set off once more. At first the going was downhill but before we reached the scene of the crash we had waded through two mountain streams, at times over our knees in the freezing, bubbling water, and climbed another ridge over two thousand feet up the mountain-side.

It was almost 3 a.m. when my nostrils caught the smell of burning. Both George and I covered a large area but although the smell grew stronger in some parts, then faded, we were unable to find any trace of the Anson or the bodies of the crew. We decided to abandon any further searching until daybreak and with other members of the party who had now joined us set off for the shepherd's cottage.

Over twenty of the search party had found the going too tough and along with my seventeen remaining companions I spent what was left of the night fast asleep on the warm dry piles of hay in the stone barn beside the cottage.

Next morning when I stood in the doorway of the barn I was able to see a large black patch farther up the mountain and quite a distance along the ridge we had searched in the darkness. When we reached it we found that the Anson was completely burned out. The wreckage lay twisted and horribly mangled in a hundred different heaps strewn among the scree and boulders. It was obvious that the aircraft had flown straight into the peak above our heads, then burst into flames. This was the Anson accounted for, but where was the missing Tiger Moth?

Bill Jennens and a small advance party, who had reached the wreckage before me, shouted that I should have a look over the crest of a knoll several hundred yards away. I did this and saw the Tiger Moth severely bent and buckled, sprawled on the rocks with its tail, still in one piece, leaning at an angle towards the sky. Pete and his colleague had had a miraculous escape and were already on their way to safety down the other side of the mountain. I heard later that he had been drawn in on top of Douglas's wreckage by a series of turbulent down-draughts.

Apart from several of the navigation instruments and log books there was little to salvage from the wrecked Anson, but for some reason, which I never fully understood, Bill insisted on bringing back the instrument panels from the Tiger Moth. The unpleasant task of preparing the bodies for transit back to the waiting vehicles was completed and we were ready to make our descent.

With one of the panels from the Tiger Moth hanging round my neck I took my turn to carry one of the stretchers. It was even harder to get down the mountainside and we had many pauses so that we could rest. Through the two rushing torrents, up the side of the second slope, past the four hundred foot drop where George had been gaily waving his torch on the previous night, we stumbled in silence, always conscious of the tragic load we carried on our stretchers.

We had been on the mountain for twenty-four hours but when I climbed into one of the lorries, ready for the journey back to Prestwick, it seemed as though we had been walking for twenty-four years.

A court of enquiry was held in an effort to establish the cause of the accident which had happened to an extremely able pilot. It was learned that the wind had been blowing much more strongly than had been forecast. Douglas, flying north towards his final turning point at Kilmarnock, had not appreciated that he was flying so far inland. It had been a particularly black night and illuminated landmarks were few and far between in that area. There had also been heavy rain squalls, a hazard for any pilot about to make his descent. Presumably Douglas had been following his usual method of steering the courses worked out for him by one of his pupils and had allowed the Anson to stray further from its track than he realized.

Whatever happened he certainly was unaware that he was flying among those treacherous hills, because the clocks found in the wreckage had both stopped only minutes after he had sent a W/T message to say that all was well and that his position was only a few miles south of Girvan—a town on the coast situated nearly twenty miles west of where the aircraft was eventually found.

Shortly after this tragic event I became engaged to Margaret Croll, a girl whom I had known for many years and with whom I had done much sailing on the Clyde. The Croll family, consisting of James Croll and his three daughters, had distinguished itself for many years in Clyde yachting regattas, and Margaret and her two sisters, Ruth and Joan, had even succeeded in winning the Coronation Cup on the Clyde in 1937, sailing their own Loch Long yacht, *Rumajo*. The boat was, in fact, the first to be built and my father-in-law had designed this popular class a few years beforehand. It is well worth noting that the cost in those days was only sixty pounds a boat, complete with sails, whereas a Loch Long boat can now cost many hundreds of pounds. Nevertheless, I'm sure her father would have been much happier if his daughter had married a nautical gentleman, but in the long run my shaky status as an amateur yachtsman won through and he eventually accepted me, as my future wife did, for better or for worse.

In mid-summer of 1939 the Central Scotland Airport at Grangemouth was completed and ready for the official opening ceremony. Scottish Aviation Ltd. had taken the lead again in constructing this modern airport in an endeavour to serve the aviation needs of both Edinburgh and Glasgow with one good airport. The Father of the Royal Air Force, Lord Trenchard, and his wife were asked to perform the opening ceremony and many notables were present, including Mr. Plesman, managing director of K.L.M., who flew over from Holland in a Douglas D.C.3, the first one I had seen, bringing with him some other senior K.L.M. officials, including Captain Spry-Leverton and his chief air hostess, Miss Baukampf.

In order to get away from the usual routine of cutting a tape or unlocking a door to signify that the place was officially open, a scheme was evolved where Lord Trenchard would rotate the propeller of a small silver model aircraft which would be wired up to a smoke generator placed outside the main airport building.

When the propeller was rotated an electrical contact was to be made which would set off the smoke from the generator.

Lined up at the far side of the airfield were a number of Hawker Hart and Hind aircraft which, on receiving the smoke signal, were to take off in formation in the direction of the main building. What happened when the whole thing was set in motion was even better than had been anticipated. The mechanical side worked so well that the smoke generator, as though sensing that this was an event of some significance, belched forth in such factory-like fashion that the far side of the airfield was completely obscured from the vision of those of us standing in the upstairs room of the building.

Great clouds of thick smoke billowed upwards and drifted across the airfield and many of those present were sure that a monstrous fire had started. The aircraft took off on cue but were over the building in their precision flypast and out of sight before anyone noticed them, so thick was the smoke screen.

Grangemouth, as a civil airport, never really got going properly before the Second World War broke out and it was a coincidence that it was only a few months after it was officially opened that I was back there again—but this time under vastly different circumstances.

The war was on and I had, by then, been called up for service with 602 Squadron which was moved to Grangemouth at the beginning of October. No longer was the airport building a thing of beauty adorned in its mantle of white, nor were the well-kept grass verges, bordering their trim flower beds, untrodden on except by their jealous keepers—the gardeners.

The building was now bedaubed with olive green, and earth-coloured camouflage, refuellers, lorries, stores and other warlike equipment lay stacked on the once tidy flower beds. The gardeners themselves were gone—gone to fight yet another war.

5 No friendly star to guide me

During the very early days of the war the R.A.F. had no night fighter squadrons. Actually it was not until late 1940 that the first specially equipped night aircraft came into being. As a result the day squadrons had to maintain both day and night watches which imposed a considerable strain on the more experienced members. Owing to a shortage of pilots trained to fly at night it always happened that the same few found themselves on the night patrols. It was also obvious that because these men had all the necessary experience they were best equipped to lead formations during daylight sorties. This exhausting state of affairs was to continue until we were well through the Battle of Britain.

One night towards the end of September, 1939, a few days before my move to Grangemouth, I found myself on standby at Abbotsinch ready to be first off in the event of a patrol being required. As a thick, damp fog hung over the airfield, reducing horizontal visibility to well below one thousand yards, I took it for granted that my services would not be required. Whistling to myself I pulled on my pyjamas before going to sleep in our tent which was pitched on the far side of the airfield near the aircraft dispersal.

The soul-destroying jangle of the telephone woke me up. I looked at my watch in the torch light. Two o'clock. I picked up the phone and heard the voice of the Controller. 'One aircraft is to patrol Abbotsinch at four thousand feet.'

I couldn't believe my ears and asked for the message to be repeated. When I put down the receiver I cursed aloud. At this

time we had no option but to comply with such orders. It was
not until later that a pilot was allowed to use his own judgement
as to whether or not he considered weather conditions to be
suitable for flying.

As quickly as I could I pulled on a pair of trousers over my
pyjamas and hastily donning my heavy uniform greatcoat
dashed out into the swirling fog. The grey clinging mass seemed
to come at me in great waves and it took some time to find my
aircraft parked in the murky darkness. Putting on my parachute
and flying helmet I climbed aboard.

George Pinkerton, my Flight Commander, who was sharing
the tent with me, was running around issuing orders to ground
crew members. Someone shouted that there were no flares in
position on the runway. Yelling something, George jumped into
his car and drove out to the windward side of the airfield. There,
he positioned his car with the headlights on. When I moved off
and took up my position ready for take-off I could just see the
tiny beams of light somewhere in the distance ahead of me. It did
the trick all the same and I was airborne, using my instruments
to clear all the many obstructions erected around the airfield.

Climbing to the specified four thousand feet I started to
circle what I imagined would be the airfield. Unfortunately the
fog belt extended to even this height and I could see nothing
below me. Pushing upwards I took my Spitfire to ten thousand
feet. I was unable to distinguish anything beneath me and it was
impossible to find a horizon by which to gauge the altitude of
my aircraft. I found also that my radio was useless. It was one
of the earlier pattern high-frequency sets, which were never very
satisfactory. The only intelligible noise which came through my
headphones was some dance music from a foreign broadcasting
station.

I was now growing worried. My greatest fear was of the
balloon barrage which floated over Glasgow. I knew that some
of the balloons were flying from positions only a mile away
from Abbotsinch. Their operational height was twelve thousand
feet.

I considered it futile to attempt to find the suspected 'raid' and set course south-west in the hope of finding clearer atmosphere around Prestwick. After twenty minutes I was still unable to distinguish anything, not even an occasional friendly star. I decided to turn back. Fifteen minutes later and still hopelessly lost I made up my mind that an emergency landing was called for as soon as was possible.

Descending to three thousand feet I released my one and only parachute flare. It spluttered several times before bursting to throw an enormous bright orange glow over the sky. Diving below the glow I was able to make out some open countryside. At least I was not heading for a built-up area. Down I went and was able to select a large field which looked suitable for what I had in mind.

I quickly lowered the undercarriage and landing flaps. Everything went smoothly. The fog had cleared up considerably and I complimented myself on having found such a smooth field for my landing. It would be a piece of cake getting in here, I thought. Down . . . down . . . I went, the Spitfire responding to my every command. Nearer and nearer came the field. Then, to my horror, I saw that what I had thought was well cropped grass was, in fact, water. I was attempting to land on one of the many small lochs and reservoirs which abound in Renfrewshire.

I hastily pumped up the wheels again and climbed back to three thousand feet, feeling the sweat running down my back and from my armpits. I then started to search for a proper field and while in the middle of this the flare burned itself out. Left alone in the darkness I didn't know what to do. I was asked later why I had not taken my parachute and baled out. To be frank the thought never even entered my head.

I turned off the fuel and let the engine run itself out, switched off and lowered the flaps. The Spitfire then glided forward with its undercarriage retracted, moving through the air like a graceful bird. I saw by the altimeter that I was still two thousand feet up. As I peered at the small glass face of the dial and pondered on my predicament I caught the shadow of something large and black loom up in front.

I yelled out at the top of my voice and in the same moment yanked hard back on the stick. There was a great tearing noise and a shudder ran through the length of the fuselage. It was fortunate that I had tightened my safety harness beforehand, saving myself from being jerked forward to hit my head on the gunsight fixed at eye-level inside the cockpit.

The Spitfire bumped and crashed across the obstructions in its path. The floor of the cockpit split open as it tore over a succession of jagged rocks. Showers of mud and gravel sprayed up to engulf me. A screech of twisting metal told me that the starboard wing had hit a heap of boulders. The force swung the aircraft round and I hit my head with a fearful whack on the side of the windscreen. Half choked by the deluge of mud and almost blinded by the blow to my head only one thought remained clear in my head: 'Is this what it's like to be killed?' Another loud crash, followed by more mud and small stones and the Spitfire came to a halt. I had made a pancake landing on top of a mountain.

I undid the quick release catches of my harness and parachute and jumped down from the cockpit. Determined to get as far away as possible from the aircraft in case it should explode I slithered and stumbled for almost two hundred yards. I threw myself into the mud and lay waiting for the blast as the fuel ignited. But nothing happened. Eventually I sat up, my head still throbbing.

When I realized I was safe and began to appreciate the predicament I was in I simply sat back and laughed to myself. Here I was in my pyjamas, on top of a mountain somewhere in Scotland. I had no idea of my whereabouts; it was pitch dark and bitterly cold. Worst of all I had no cigarettes.

As I took stock of my situation the sound of a motor horn rent the air. I looked round. The noise seemed to be coming from the direction of my crashed Spitfire. I wandered back and found that it was the undercarriage warning horn blaring forth its message. I pushed the throttle forward to stop the ear-splitting racket.

It was then an awful thought ran through my head. I had

committed two dastardly breaches of the law. Firstly, I had shown a light in the blackout. I was positive that the flare must have lit up the half of Renfrewshire. Secondly, I had blown a horn after 11 p.m.

I had a fresh look at my battered Spitfire and decided to climb back into the cockpit. Switching on the navigation lights in the hope that they might be spotted from below I settled down to read a book which I found in one of the pockets of my greatcoat. The amber glow from the cockpit lights was sufficient to enable me to see the pages, but forty-five minutes later when I heard a noise outside I found that I was still gazing at the first page. I must have dozed off.

Startled by a clatter from beside the fuselage I jumped to my feet. A double-barrelled shotgun was levelled at my head. A voice in the gloom demanded: 'Who are you?'

I just couldn't answer. For the life of me I couldn't remember my own name. The voice demanded an answer. The gun waved menacingly. I tried to think. Eventually I croaked a reply: 'Me.'

'Who the devil is me?' demanded the voice. 'Come out and let me have a look at you.' I clambered out of the cockpit and saw a tall man glowering at me. As I landed on the ground he noticed the R.A.F. greatcoat and lowered the shotgun. He laughed and I found myself joining in.

'Good God, man, I thought you were a Hun who had been shot down,' he managed to blurt out, between fits of laughing and coughing.

As my rescuer led me away from the aircraft he told me his name was McColl and that he was keeper of the reservoirs in the area of Lochwinnoch. Most likely he was responsible for the one into which I had nearly taken a headlong dive. He had seen the flare dropping and heard the scream of my engine as I had climbed away after my attempt at landing. A little later he had heard the sound of the Spitfire crashing into the top of the mountain. Getting his gun from the house he had made a tortuous climb up to the summit fully expecting to arrest a German pilot.

By the time he had finished his story we had reached his house, which stood in an isolated position on the main slope of the mountain. A meal of tea, bacon and eggs and a very welcome cigarette soon sent a warm glow running through me.

Later in the day I found myself back at Abbotsinch going over the story of my exploits to my Flight Commander. When the interview was over I asked him if anything had come of the suspected 'raid' which I had been sent up to investigate. He laughed and handed me a cigarette.

'No need to worry yourself over that. The unidentified aircraft was only one of our own bombers which had gone off course.'

A little over a fortnight later, on Monday, October 16, I took off from Drem Aerodrome in the company of two other Spitfires to intercept a 'bogey', or unidentified aircraft, which our radar stations had picked up as it approached the Scottish coast from the east.

We wheeled northwards and kept our eyes skinned for first sighting of the mystery aircraft which, the Fighter Controller assured us, was now six miles ahead and turning north. Seeking and probing, sweeping in and out of the hundreds of rain clouds scattered over the North Sea, we pursued our game of cat and mouse. A great deal was at stake. We were hell bent on being the first members of 602 Squadron to intercept a German aircraft.

'Bogey has turned North . . . North . . . due North. Buster . . . Buster.' The Controller's voice carried a deliberate air of urgency. Douglas Farquhar, who was leading the section, responded to the cry of 'Buster' and piled on the speed. Within seconds we were forcing on after our invisible target at nearly four hundred miles per hour. After holding our course for a further ten minutes without further news or any sight of our quarry, whose plot had faded from the Operations Room table, we headed southwards and back to Drem.

We were all feeling a little bit disgruntled. What we had just done had been the exact same pattern we had been following for several weeks. We were now suspicious that the radar stations at Drone Hill and St. Abbs Head were only reporting spoof echoes. The only aggressive objects we had ever encountered during our many mad 'scrambles' had been flocks of wild geese.

c

Douglas decided, however, to continue our patrol and land at Leuchars, an airfield under Coastal Command's control. The ground crews stationed there were trained to handle Lockheed Hudson and Avro Anson aircraft. Spitfires were a new breed of aircraft as far as they were concerned and as we reckoned they would need about thirty minutes to carry out the refuelling procedure and replenish the oxygen we decided there was time to have a quick bite to eat.

The first spoonful of soup was barely in my mouth when the station's air raid warning system whined into life. Our table companion threw down his cutlery.

'Blast it,' he shouted. 'This is the third practice alert we've had today. The Old Man is a real stickler for making these practices as authentic as possible. Come on—you'd all better follow me and I'll take you to the shelter.'

The air raid shelter was full so we all climbed up on top of the mound of grass and lay there. I munched a roll which I had swiftly lifted as we hurried from the mess. After several minutes I heard the sound of aircraft away in the distance. A little later I saw two flying up the estuary towards Edinburgh. They seemed to be at about eight thousand feet and were constantly being obscured by heavy clouds rolling in from the sea.

'Blenheims,' shouted Douglas. 'I wonder where they're making for?'

'It looks like a new make of Blenheim to me,' I said. I felt my stomach rumble and sat up. 'Look, I'm hungry.'

Douglas got to his feet. 'I'll just nip over to the mess and find out what's going on and see how long we are going to be stuck here.' He strode off towards the side entrance and disappeared inside.

When he reappeared less than a minute later he was red-faced and waving his arms around.

'For God's sake, come on. We're a right bunch of bloody fools. These are no Blenheims—they're JU 88's.'

A little van was waiting to take us back to the airfield. Cutting corners and careering across the grass verges we arrived on the tarmac to find that the Coastal Command lads had not only completed the refuelling but had started up the Spitfires into the bargain. As we ran across to clamber in I saw Group Captain Brian Baker, the Station Commander—the Old Man himself—shouting at us. In the confusion I gathered that the general tone of his remarks dealt with the incompetency of Fighter Command in general and three pilots of 602 Squadron in particular.

Unknown to us, at the time while we had been idling away the minutes on the roof of the shelter, the rest of 602 and 603 Squadrons, the latter still flying Gloster Gladiators, were piling into over a dozen German KG 100 bombers attempting to attack the Naval dockyards at Rosyth. This was, in fact, the first German raid over the British Isles. Subsequent records were to show that this particular Luftwaffe squadron, equipped with JU 88 aircraft, comprised a carefully selected bunch of aircrew, ex-German airline pilots, graduates at British universities and so on—but all having some personal knowledge of the target areas they were briefed to attack.

They were briefed carefully to avoid dropping any bombs on land-based targets to prevent casualties to civilians. They followed their instructions to the letter—no bombs fell on land. The only casualties were sustained by a Naval cruiser, anchored to the west of the Forth Railway Bridge.

However, I'm certain that a number of pedestrians on the outskirts of Edinburgh and Leith must have been in no little danger when the occasional JU 88 was being hotly pursued by a Spitfire or Gladiator at rooftop level in a hail of ·303 fire between the fighters and the rear-gunners of the hunted bombers.

The only casualties were four of the JU 88's and a reconnaissance Heinkel which came to grief in the sea off the Lothian coast. Several of the German crews were picked up and nursed back to health in local hospitals before being shipped off to Canada where they were interned. Among them was the pilot of one of the JU 88's who had been a student at Edinburgh University and a member of the flying club at Macmerry prior to the outbreak of war. Some of our lads were allowed to visit their victims in hospital and the story was told of how this young pilot's main worry was that his former girl friend in Edinburgh should never find out what he had been up to that day.

However, to get back to my own part in the affairs of that October afternoon. We three tail-end Charleys eventually got ourselves into the air and took off amid ribald cheering from the Coastal Command ground crews. We headed towards the scene of the fighting.

Crossing the Firth I was immediately mistaken for an enemy aircraft and fired on by the aircraft carrier *Furious* which was zig-zagging up and down the river at high speed to avoid becoming a bombing casualty herself. I took swift action to avoid the unwelcome attentions of our own Naval guns and arrived in the area near the Forth Bridge. To my disappointment I found that the skirmish was almost over. My only contribution to the effort consisted of one very long-range, and equally ineffectual, burst at a fast departing JU 88 as it climbed for the safety of the clouds out over the coast.

Although it was considerably closer than my first sighting of it off Leuchars it still looked like a Blenheim to me. All the same, this fight over the Forth was the first direct confrontation between British and German aircraft over Britain itself. Before many months passed such aerial warfare was to become commonplace.

6　Mistaken identity

After they had broken the ice with us by their raid on the Firth of Forth the Germans continued to send a steady supply of reconnaissance aircraft, intermingled with the odd raider, to harry the defences in the North-East in general and 603 Squadron and ourselves in particular. Because of this we found ourselves in the enviable position of seeing more real action in the space of a few weeks than the rest of Fighter Command squadrons put together had seen since the war began. In fact by early 1940 we were rapidly becoming looked upon as 'the experts'.

About this time a single prototype Spitfire, armed with two 9 mm. cannons in place of the conventional eight Browning ·303 guns, made its appearance and, in view of the better chances offered to show its effectiveness in action, the Air Ministry arranged for it to be loaned to 602 Squadron as soon as it had completed its manufacturer's trials. From the day of its arrival we flew it as the number two aircraft in whichever section happened to be keeping the readiness state.

In the course of a patrol led by Douglas Farquhar, the section intercepted a Heinkel 111 as it approached the East Coast and Douglas immediately waded in to the attack and managed to silence the rear-gunner's return fire. Calling on George Proudman, the pilot of the cannon-armed Spitfire, to go in and do his damnedest with the new type of armament, he pulled to one side to observe the results.

George blazed away with the cannons and had the satisfaction of seeing large chunks of the Heinkel breaking away and a tell-tale streak of black smoke pour from its starboard engine.

Seeking to land as quickly as possible the Nazi pilot made for the nearest bit of solid ground in sight and carried out a hurried forced landing with his undercarriage retracted. This happened on a particularly deserted headland not far from St. Abbs Head.

Douglas was especially anxious to have this prize preserved from sabotage in order to assess, more accurately, the value of the cannon, as opposed to machine-gun fire, and did all he could to attract the attention of someone on the ground to the fate of the Heinkel. However, the few inhabitants of these parts were already immune to the noise of low-flying Spitfires due to the amount of practices carried out in that area and had long ceased to bother about aerial activity in the sky above them.

Nothing daunted, therefore, Douglas decided that the only thing to do was to land close beside his prey and do what he could to stop the Germans from destroying the vital evidence.

The Heinkel slithered to a stop on top of a high knoll and there appeared to be a reasonably flat piece of ground running along its foot. Douglas lowered his undercarriage and made a perfect three-point touch down not far from the crippled bomber. At this point his luck deserted him, however, for as soon as the wheels of his Spitfire touched the ground, he realized all too late that the surface was extremely marshy.

There was nothing he could do about it—over he went, aircraft and all, coming to rest upside down in the middle of a bog. The mud oozed and bubbled under the weight of the Spitfire and the more he struggled in the cockpit the further the aircraft sank into the swamp.

While suspended inverted, with the mud already halfway up, or rather down, his forehead, Douglas suddenly felt the aircraft being forced up at one side and a couple of friendly arms appeared in the gloom to assist him to extricate himself from his involuntary sloth-like posture. At least this is what it appeared like to Douglas. However, when he eventually succeeded in wriggling out from under his capsized aircraft, with the aid of some hefty pulls from the mysterious pair of arms, he found his rescuers were not friendly local people. Far from it—they were members of the crew of the enemy bomber which had been so recently despatched.

Wasting no time, although utterly amazed, Douglas, in his best schoolboy German, proceeded formally to arrest this alien crew—all three—and demanded the immediate surrender of their personal firearms. But the Germans refused to have any of his nonsense and refused point blank to part with their weapons. There was very little Douglas could do about it—he was unarmed and outnumbered.

Slightly huffed, Douglas and the Germans made their way up the slope to where the Heinkel, having been already well set alight by its crew, was a blazing inferno of white-hot metal, exploding ammunition and signals cartridges. He helped them to move the injured rear-gunner to a safer spot, all the time arguing that they should surrender to him while the going was good.

About fifteen minutes elapsed before a detachment of Local Defence Volunteers (the Home Guard was not formed until several months later) appeared over a rise some distance away. Douglas took this opportunity to make another effort to get the prized Mausers from the opposition.

'Look,' he shouted, pointing to the band of khaki-clad figures threading their way across a nearby field, rifles at the port position. 'If you're captured with those revolvers on you it will make it all the harder for you in the long run,' he attempted to explain in his halting German.

The Germans took a long, hard look at the advancing soldiers and quickly handed over their automatics. A few minutes later the soldiers arrived and the officer-in-charge walked straight up to Douglas, for some reason, and announced: 'You are my prisoners. Put your hands above your heads and don't move.'

Douglas obeyed, along with the Germans, and in no time the worthy volunteers were frisking their captives for hidden weapons. Douglas soon found himself the object of special attention when his newly-won armoury was discovered. He was quickly relieved of his load. By this time Douglas realized that the volunteers were mistaking him for a member of the Heinkel's crew as the Spitfire was completely hidden from view below the dip in the ground. Having a pawkish sense of humour, here was a situation too good for him to miss.

'Do any of you speak English?' enquired the officer.

'I often try to,' replied Douglas, putting on a phoney guttural accent.

'Let me see your identity papers then,' requested his captor.

The only piece of paper Douglas had in his pockets was his income tax return. He fished it out and handed it over.

The officer took one glance and recoiled a couple of paces when he saw the familiar looking document. Losing quite a bit of his dignity he shouted excitedly to a companion: 'Hey, Bertie—look at this—this form is just like ours. These blokes must have been meaning to plant a spy on us.'

He turned to face his prisoners once more. 'Right, you lot, go and give your chum a helping hand . . .' he gesticulated to where the injured German lay on the grass . . . 'and then line up over here.'

The Germans, by this time, however, had guessed that Douglas was being mistaken for one of them and were none too eager to welcome him into their ranks as a fellow prisoner.

Waving their arms around and shouting loudly they did their best to disclaim any friendly feelings for their erstwhile captor and insisted on having nothing to do with him.

The soldiers looked on in astonishment as they saw the feud erupting between their prisoners. Douglas shouted back and all this added to the confusion. Gesticulating violently the Germans attracted the attention of the guard captain who strode over to put an end to their unruly behaviour. One of them took him by the arm and led him over to the edge of the rise. He pointed to the inverted Spitfire, just barely visible in the middle of the bog.

This only served to complicate matters. The officer, taking it for granted that the pilot was trapped in the wreckage called on some of his men and set off down the hill at a jog-trot to carry out a rescue of the British pilot.

The Germans still milled about on top of the hill almost

beside themselves with frustration as they saw the soldiers take off at high speed towards the Spitfire and not taking any notice fo Douglas who was finding it hard to keep a straight face as the pantomime around him grew better each minute.

He walked to the edge of the hill. A few of the volunteers left on guard moved after their 'spy'. As the Germans saw him draw near they moved away—anxious to avoid any contact with their masquerading companion. Down in the marsh the guard officer and his men were up to their thighs in slime and mud, trying to shift the aircraft. Eventually they were able to peer inside the cockpit. It was empty. Perplexed, the officer straightened his back. Where had the pilot got to?

Douglas decided the joke had gone far enough and walked down the hill to confront the officer with the news that he was the Spitfire pilot and not, as the soldier had thought, a spy flown in from Germany. It took him some time to convince the soldiers, who were now tired and weary from the shouting that had gone on and the physical effort of trying to shift the Spitfire from the marsh. However, he succeeded and after a few oaths aimed in his direction they appreciated the joke and returned Douglas to the base at Drem in comfort and without too much delay.

King George VI visited us at Drem less than two weeks later and awarded the Distinguished Flying Cross to Douglas at a simple ceremony held on the tarmac in front of the assembled squadrons. He was obviously very amused by the story as he spoke about it to me a year later when I had the honour of lunching with their Majesties during a subsequent visit to Scotland. In slightly less exalted circles, however, a less lenient view was taken of Douglas's escapade. Senior officers were quick to issue orders prohibiting anyone from landing alongside their vanquished foes. Spitfires, they maintained, were not all that expendable—neither, for that matter, were fully trained fighter pilots.

In January, 1940, Margaret and I were married and I was given the opportunity of fourteen days' leave.

For more than the obvious reason I shall never forget that

day, for it coincided with the start of one of the worst snow storms in living memory. Large flakes were falling as we left the wedding reception in Glasgow to drive the thirty miles to Troon, our intended stopping-off place for the first night of the honeymoon.

The volume of snow increased unrelentingly as we drove across Fenwick Moor in my faithful old Vauxhall and I was thankful that I had recently fitted a fog lamp to it as the masked headlights did little to penetrate the gloom of the seemingly endless wall of white. Eventually, more by good luck than good judgement, we slithered to a halt in front of the Marine Hotel and made our way inside.

Next morning there was no sign of the car—nor indeed of the flight of steps leading up to the hotel. The entire countryside around us was clothed in a mantle of snow to an average depth of seven or eight feet. We learned later that we were almost the last car to get over the Moor road for nearly ten days and that a fellow motorist, who had set out from Glasgow only a few minutes after our departure, had been dug out days later, having suffocated in his car while awaiting rescue.

In some cases even the telegraph poles had disappeared under the snow and it was obvious we were destined to spend our honeymoon on the Ayrshire coast, whether we wanted to or not. But under the circumstances, who were we to care?

Not long after I returned to my unit, we received orders to move the Squadron once more—this time we were to split forces. 'A' Flight was to be based at Montrose while 'B' Flight, of which I was by now Flight Commander, was to move to Dyce, about seven miles north of Aberdeen.

Douglas Farquhar had been promoted to the rank of Wing Commander and posted to command a fighter station on the south-east coast of England. George Pinkerton had returned as Commanding Officer and he was to base himself at Dyce with us.

The northern aerodrome was a quagmire. No other word could describe it, and the only strip on which it was possible to land was one of about four hundred yards in length and about twenty yards wide, composed of tar camouflage markings, which were intended to give the effect of hedgerows when viewed from above.

We set up our headquarters in the old Aberdeen Flying Club premises situated on the opposite side of the airfield from the main R.A.F. building, which were occupied by units of Coastal Command.

Later, it was decided to add a proper Fighter Command operations room and we were inundated with joiners, carpenters, painters and a veritable army of Post Office engineers. Owing to a shortage of telephone switchboards we had to make do with individual telephones and at one time were the proud possessors of no fewer than twenty-three such instruments, all alike and placed along the newly constructed dais.

This was fine and looked very imposing until one of them rang. Then it was sheer pandemonium trying to find out which one it was. If two rang together we just gave up, for by the time half of the hand pieces had been replaced on the wrong bases due to the haste adopted, the caller had given up and rung off.

There was one telephone we could not fathom all the same. This was the twenty-third in the line and it was set a little apart from the others. Many times in an effort to discover to where the instrument was connected we turned the small handle but got no reply. After it had been lying in its aloof and rather lonely position for more than three weeks, the mystery of its connections having not yet been unravelled, it suddenly burst forth, ringing shrilly.

Archie McKellar happened to be near by and picked up the receiver while we all crowded round eager to hear the voice of the mystery caller.

'This is the A.O.C.,' said a voice in the distance, but loud enough for most of us to hear as we looked over Archie's shoulder.

'Oh yes,' replied our companion, 'well, this is the King of Siam here. How do you do?'

For a second or two there was silence and I could hear someone taking a deep breath. Then came the angry shout.

'Dammit, you young whippersnapper. Who are you anyway? Do you realize who you are talking to?'

Archie was still not certain but guessed that the excited, spluttering voice coming from the earpiece must have quite a bit of rank judging by the noise it was making.

'I'm sorry—I couldn't quite catch that,' said Archie quietly.

This time the silence was even longer. When the voice came through once more it was, by now, calm and collected and speaking very deliberately so that no one could possibly make any mistakes.

'This is Air Vice-Marshal R. E. Saul—can you understand that? Now do you know to whom you are speaking?'

Quick as a flash, Archie muttered in the affirmative and added: 'Do you know to whom *you* are speaking?'

'No.'

'Thank goodness for that,' replied Archie, as he hastily replaced the receiver.

There was a rueful smile on his face. 'That must be a direct line to the A.O.C. Imagine that—what a hell of a way to find out.'

When Air Vice-Marshal Saul next visited us we explained in full what had happened and he laughed just as much as we had done over our frightful mistake.

A somewhat similar incident occurred over a teleprinter which was set up in our crew room—there being no room for it in the Operations Room. A charming little W.A.A.F. invaded the sanctuary of this room early one morning while those of us not at readiness were still lolling around in our pyjamas. She strode over to the machine and with only a curt nod in our general direction sat down on a chair placed in front of it.

All day long she sat there, except for a break for lunch. Next morning she was back again and took up her position as before. Although we made various attempts at conversation she was either extremely shy or didn't want to have anything to do with us. Certainly she didn't give us a great deal of encouragement. Late that afternoon, after her second day of silent vigil, one of the Post Office engineers happened to see her sitting there patiently waiting.

He walked over. 'What are you doing there?' he asked.

'Waiting for any messages to come through from Group,' she replied demurely.

The man threw back his head and laughed. He clutched his sides and his antics made us look up. When he had recovered he turned to the girl who was ignoring him after his outburst of mirth.

His voice trembled as he told her: 'Well, I'm afraid you'll have a long wait, miss. You see it's not connected up at the other end yet.'

There was silence in the room. The girl stared at him, her mouth hanging open in amazement. For a moment it looked as if she would burst into tears. Grimly, she got to her feet, picked up her bag and with shoulders straight marched out of the room amid gales of laughter.

Like the twenty-third telephone this teleprinting device remained mute and mysterious for many more days. While we were having afternoon tea about a week later it suddenly burst into life and clattered away like a demented typist. Everyone made a dive for it and gathered round to see what was being said. But the hieroglyphics on the roll of paper were quite unintelligible to us.

Waiting until it came to rest, one of my companions, who claimed to have some knowledge of how such a machine operated, tapped back: 'Are you a blonde or brunette?'

For almost ten seconds the machine remained quiet. The operator had no doubt decided to ignore this leading question. All at once it started to clatter again.

'I am an airman,' spat back the machine with more venom than we imagined possible from such an impersonal lump of steel.

7 Marksmanship at any price

The personal air raid shelter which I had gone to great pains to construct at the bottom of the garden had once been a pigsty. After several sojourns in its rather smelly interior my wife remarked: 'I'd rather be blown to Kingdom Come than have to spend another night in this confounded place.' Such was my thanks.

By now it was mid-June, 1940, and the war was well under way.

Margaret and I had been married for over four months but it had not been possible for her to live near me owing to the Squadron's continual journeyings between the North and South of Scotland. However, the A.O.C.'s wife, Claire, had rented a trim little cottage at Gullane in East Lothian for several months and had invited Margaret to stay with her for a while during the squadron's latest stint on the near-by airfield at Drem.

Although I was unable to live out with her, at least I was able to spend my free time down at the cottage and it was during one of these happy occasions that I hit upon the idea of sandbagging the old pigsty in order to provide a modicum of protection for the girls if the Germans ever decided to have a go at Drem, which was less than a mile from where the cottage stood.

The German armies had already marched the length and breadth of Western Europe. Now only Britain remained inviolate in the face of what seemed to be impossible odds.

We were getting plenty of opportunities to improve our techniques in aerial fighting. Back now at Drem, once more, the squadron's morale was high. Radar cover was now vastly improved as too was the standard of fighter controlling. Night after night we maintained our state of readiness and around midnight on one occasion I found myself patrolling at about ten thousand feet on a line between Dalkeith and Musselburgh, both of which positions were marked by two coloured searchlights. There was a considerable noise on the radio and I gathered we were on to something. From time to time the voices of other pilots came through to me together with the Controller's urgent appeals to 'look to port', 'Buster', or 'It's dead ahead of you now'.

There seemed to be a great deal of activity to the east of me but I was forced to focus my attention on the west. Back and forth I went, turning every five minutes or so as I reached the extremities of my patrol line. There was a slight haze in the air and the coloured lights which marked my turning points showed up like long coloured pencils pointing vertically into the sky. The urgent chatter continued. They were certainly having fun to the west of Edinburgh.

I saw three searchlights suddenly burst into action about two miles to the north. Within seconds their powerful beams had converged to form a tripod of light. There, caught like a trapped moth and glistening like a star, sat a silvery-grey aircraft.

I couldn't believe my eyes. There had been no word of 'bogeys' or 'bandits' being anywhere near me. I convinced myself that the lights had picked up one of our own boys. Opening wide the throttle I raced towards the concentration of light. I turned the firing ring from 'safe' to 'fire' just in case . . .

As I closed in on the aircraft, still brilliantly illuminated in the searchlights' glare, I saw the black swastika painted on the large rounded fin and rudder. It was a Heinkel 111. The German aircraft was heaving around—the pilot trying to take all positive evasive action to get away from the lights. But the men on the ground were having none of it. They hung on to their Heinkel and gave me ample opportunity to get it lined up in my sights.

I squeezed the firing button and the Spitfire shuddered as the light Brownings spat out their lethal load. I was now overtaking the Heinkel so fast that I had to pull away violently to avoid colliding with it. As I fell away in a steep dive I had no time to see whether or not I had inflicted any damage on my quarry.

Being so excited at the chance to make my first kill I had completely forgotten to close my throttle and found myself hurtling downwards through the coal-black sky at a fearful rate. I had no idea what my flying attitude was as most of the instruments on the panel seemed to have gone crazy. The cross bar of the artificial horizon was stuck tight in the top left hand corner of the instrument face; the gyro-compass was spinning round so fast that it was impossible to take a reading and the altimeter was unwinding itself like a clock gone mad. As the dive increased I felt a great weight pressing on my shoulders. I could feel panic starting to well up inside me and did my best to suppress it.

I tried to move the rudder pedals. I couldn't find them. Side to side I swept my feet. There was no trace of the two control bars. I tried hard to understand what was happening and was almost sick when the Spitfire tumbled around and fell in an air pocket.

In the middle of this fresh buffeting the reason for my discomfort, and my inability to find the rudder pedals, struck me. I was upside down and going into a screaming inverted dive.

Wrenching on the stick and using every trick in the book, and a few more besides, I was able to turn the Spitfire over and point her upwards again. I was shaking now—partly from shock and partly from the efforts to control the aircraft.

The Spitfire was behaving normally again—the powerful throb of the engine, as I climbed, sweet music to my ears after the terror of the previous few seconds. I was amazed to see that the searchlights still surrounded the Heinkel. Luck was being more than kind to me tonight. I knew it wasn't often that a fighter pilot got a second chance at such a magnificent target.

As I closed once again, more carefully this time, I was delighted to see a thick stream of smoke pouring from the

German aircraft's starboard engine. I closed in astern of him and prepared to deliver the coup de grâce. It was almost too easy. All the same my heart pounded with excitement. I daren't make a mistake now.

My fingers trembled on the firing button but I controlled myself sufficiently until the Heinkel's full wing span filled the orange coloured image on my reflector sight. This was the moment. I squeezed the firing button and the damage was done.

As if in answer to the dominating chatter of the Spitfire's Brownings a mixture of glycol and engine oil swept back towards me from the stricken Heinkel. The thick oily stream burst on my windscreen and as I pulled away to port I was unable to see out. Eventually the mess cleared and I saw that the German was on his way down. Both engines were ablaze and great streams of smoke billowed back behind the Heinkel, which was fast losing height.

I followed my victim across the Lothian countryside as one battery of searchlights handed him over to the next. It was only when we crossed the coast, south of Dunbar, that they were finally forced to relinquish their hold on the target they had stuck to so magnificently.

My eyes were now well accustomed to the dark conditions and it was easy to follow the German's progress from the size of the flames from his blazing engines. About a mile or so out to sea he prepared to ditch and I watched the two beams from his landing lights as he switched them on in the final moments.

All of a sudden the lights seemed to vanish as the aircraft struck the sea. Then I saw them take on a greenish hue as the water closed over them. The flames died down too. I circled over the doomed aircraft. Slowly I saw the lights under the surface begin to dim. The ghostly green light still showed up from under the waves but was growing fainter every second. Soon there was nothing to see. The sea had claimed my first kill. The cold waters of the North Sea had sucked it down to its grave.

Flying low over the spot where I had seen the Heinkel sink I fired the colours of the day—a two star Very cartridge. This would mark the spot for any rescue craft which might be making its way towards the scene. The colours of the day were changed daily and a wide permutation was used. It happened to be red-red at that particular time of that particular day when I fired them off. What I didn't know was that the ground defence forces in the district had also arranged their own system of code signals against an unexpected invasion. By an unfortunate coincidence a two star red signal to them meant that the balloon was on the point of going up.

Popular as I may have been with some people that night my stock certainly went down with the Army, which turned out in force to protect our shores against the hordes of invaders at 2 a.m. in immediate response to my well-meaning attempt to direct a lifeboat to the aid of a stricken raider.

However, my efforts had not been in vain. The crew of the Heinkel were eventually picked up in their rubber dinghy, injured but alive, and sent to Edinburgh Castle for interrogation.

Upon my return to Drem I was met by a delighted bunch of my colleagues who had been able to enjoy a grandstand view of the entire proceedings. According to them I had come up to deliver my second attack just as the Heinkel, clearly visible in the beam of the searchlights, passed over Drem. 'Batchy' Atcherly, the Station Commander, had had the greatest difficulty in dissuading our ground defence guns from opening fire on it as he had realized that I was probably coming up behind. I was immensely relieved to hear of his good sense.

Flight Sergeant O'Connor, a most efficient N.C.O., who was in charge of the ground crews, came up to me, a broad grin showing up the lines on his face.

'Well done, sir, well done.' He pressed a mug of steaming tea into my hands. 'You've earned another scalp for the Flight.'

The flight sergeant shouted to a corporal who stood near by. 'Hey, Burnett—go and fetch a paint brush.'

But Corporal Burnett had already thought of that idea. He lifted up a small pot of paint and a brand new camel hair brush. 'Here, Flight,' he shouted.

Then he addressed me. 'Where do you want it put, sir?'

Next morning Spitfire LO-Q was to stand proudly in the dispersal area, a neat little swastika painted on the fuselage just below the windscreen combing.

After the welcome-back party was well under way I made for the nearest telephone and got in touch with my wife. As most of the activity had taken place in the sky above the cottage I felt sure she must have watched, with bated breath, as her husband fought off yet another German raider.

I heard the ringing tone start up. A minute went past and still there was no answer. The phone rang and rang. Finally I heard it stop as the receiver was lifted. A breathless voice said: 'Hullo, who's speaking?'

I was still excited and rushed in with my question. 'What did you think of this evening's performance then, Marg?'

'Who's that—who's speaking?' came the query.

I tried again. 'It's me—Sandy—your husband.'

'Oh it's you, is it? What do you mean? What did I think of what?'

I shouted into the telephone. 'The raid. I got one slap-bang over your head. Didn't you watch it?'

There was silence for a second or two. 'The raid. Oh no, dear, I didn't see it. I went into the shelter.'

So much for my wife as spectator. That was the one and only time she used the shelter after her remark to me about preferring to be blown up rather than spend another night in it.

One evening shortly after this escapade I slipped off unnoticed to see my wife in Gullane and was surprised to find the A.O.C. sitting in the house when I arrived. Pinkerton was on leave at the time and, being the senior Flight Commander, I was supposed to be looking after the squadron. However, surprisingly enough, the A.O.C., Air Vice-Marshal Saul, seemed quite pleased to see me and bade me sit down and have a drink.

'And how is the C.O. of the squadron?' he asked.

'As far as I know, sir, he's fine—he's on leave. Didn't you know that?' I replied.

I saw him look into his whisky glass as if taking stock of the contents.

'Well, if that's the case,' he said, 'he's absent without leave.' He drained his glass and put it down on the small table at his elbow.

'But, sir,' I started to remonstrate, 'I saw his leave chit which you yourself had approved before he went away . . .'

Before I could continue the A.O.C. held up a hand to silence me. 'Don't be an ass, Sandy,' came the unexpected reply. 'I've made you C.O. of 602 Squadron as from today. The signal will be in tomorrow.'

For once in my life I was speechless.

Not long afterwards a signal came through ordering 602 Squadron to Westhampnett and before long we were caught up in all the fury of the Battle of Britain. As the struggle for air supremacy wore on we found ourselves having to fly higher and higher to reach the German escorting fighters, which were now constant companions to almost all the bomber formations sent to drop their lethal loads over Britain in daylight.

602 Squadron being the only Spitfire unit among the three squadrons making up the Tangmere Wing, invariably had the job of flying top cover and tackling the escorts while our heavier and slightly less nippy Hurricane colleagues waded into the main bomber force. By doing this we were able to give them a clearer field in which to down the bombers.

However, we eventually found ourselves operating at heights in excess of thirty thousand feet and when we had to fly through clouds of moist air on our way up there was always a chance that some, or all, of our light Browning guns, mounted along the wings of our Spitfires, would become frozen up.

If this happened the remote firing mechanism would almost certainly fail to function at the critical moment. This could, at times, be highly embarrassing as well as extremely dangerous. It gave one a most uncomfortable feeling to find that one's guns wouldn't fire when most needed and to be chased around the sky by an angry Messerschmitt knowing that you couldn't retaliate. It was not long before we acquired the habit of giving our guns a short burst when we first sighted our quarry to make sure they had not frozen up and this helped to ward off many embarrassing encounters.

On this particular morning in August, 1940, we had taken off from Westhampnett in company with the two Tangmere squadrons and had taken up our top-cover position about a quarter of a mile astern and four to five hundred feet above the Hurricanes. In this formation we climbed on the 'vector' passed to us by the controller in the Tangmere operations room. As we passed through twenty thousand feet, 602 Squadron was vectored off on its own towards the German fighters, which on this occasion were flying as top-cover for the incoming bombers as opposed to the close escort which they more often provided.

We had passed through a number of heavy clouds on our way up and I was mindful of the possibility of ice having formed. Reaching twenty-eight thousand feet I spotted a number of twin-engined ME 110's circling around in the distance. They were at least two to three miles dead ahead of us.

'Tally Ho,' I shouted over the intercom. I turned the safety ring on the firing mechanism to the 'Fire' position. On pressing the firing button to make the usual clearance check I was startled to see one of the 110's suddenly break off from the circling gaggle ahead and make off at high speed towards the Channel.

Thick black smoke poured in great waves from its starboard engine. No one else in my formation had fired at this particular aircraft and although I did not lay any claim to it at the subsequent intelligence de-briefing 'one damaged' was awarded to me. I felt a bit of a fraud in accepting the credit for hitting the Messerschmitt. It was a pure fluke.

On another occasion I was leading the squadron in a diving attack on a number of JU 88's which were flying in a series of 'vic's' line astern. I was firing away at the centre man in the leading 'vic' without any effect. To my embarrassment, however, the leader of the second 'vic' suddenly keeled over and went down. It was a confirmed kill but I shudder when I think back on the dreadful shooting on my part that sent it spinning towards the earth.

I was to have a true moment of triumph under different circumstances not long after this. We were hanging about the dispersal area while the squadron maintained its usual state of readiness. Three rings sounded on the operations telephone. This was the signal that the whole squadron, as opposed to only one flight, was required to scramble. Books were flung aside, Mae Wests hastily pulled on and we ran out of the crew room towards our waiting Spitfires. Within three minutes all twelve aircraft were in the sky and climbing fast towards the rendezvous point.

'Buster, Villa Leader, Buster,' came the voice of our controller. 'Twelve plus bandits at Angels One Five. Now three five—thirty-five—miles south of Weymouth.'

Acknowledging this information I called the aircraft into battle formation as we roared on upwards. We were not long in reaching our patrol position and were vectored south towards the incoming raiders. The weather was quite clear and only a few scattered cumulus clouds marred the unbroken canvas of the sky. Our quarry soon hove into sight in the now familiar pattern of 'vics' of three aircraft flying in vic-line-astern.

There were about six or seven 'vics' of Dornier 17's with about a dozen ME 109 single-engined fighters providing close escort. Detailing Micky Mount who was leading 'B' Flight to cope with the fighters I swung the remaining six Spitfires into a good attacking position and bore down on the leading Dornier.

This time my firing was spot on and I did not miss. I saw the perspex roof shatter and the port engine burst into flames. Finally as I flashed through the formation in the continuation of my dive large pieces started to break off the Dornier's port wing. He was definitely a goner.

Out of the corner of my eye I could see more of our Spitfires wading into the attack on the other bombers. Before very long the German formation had scattered in all directions. Within minutes the sky seemed empty. All was quiet and peaceful again. Only white fluffy clouds drifted lazily across my field of vision.

Of course when one realizes that the relative speeds of our fighters and the Germans was anything up to 800 m.p.h. when we met head-on it was not surprising that the sky should have cleared so quickly.

During my dive I lost a considerable amount of height. When I finally pulled out I found I was down to around twelve thousand feet. Swinging my Spitfire northwards in a steep climb I concentrated hard on trying to pick up the threads of the battle. Suddenly something travelling in the same direction as I was, streaked past my starboard wing-tip. To my horror I realized that the shadow speeding past me had been a burst of tracer bullets. A quick glance in my rear-view mirror showed me that one of the 109's was firmly glued to my tail.

It has been said on many occasions that a drowning man sees his whole life flash across his vision as he goes down for the third time. I am a firm believer in this statement now. In that fraction of a minute between first seeing the tracer and then its source in the mirror every bit of instruction I had ever been given on the art of staying alive flashed across my mind.

'If you ever see a tracer coming at you then you can bet your bottom dollar it's being used as a sighter,' was one of the pearls of wisdom which jumped into my mind. If my attacker was indeed using his for this purpose then he must have been about as bad a shot as I was, for the burst had been about ten feet wide of my wing tip.

Opening my throttle to its limit I pulled the stick back until my sturdy little Spitfire was literally sitting on its tail. Simultaneously I side-slipped towards the tracer. My hunch proved to be correct. The German's next furious burst was equally as far off my port wing tip. I can well imagine the terrible frustration being suffered at that moment by my opposite number in the Luftwaffe. Had I not myself been equally ineffective on so many occasions?

My second attempt to side-slip produced instead a quite involuntary stall turn to port. By now my faithful Spitfire was running out of forward speed due to my attempts to climb so steeply. This manoeuvre seemed to surprise my pursuer just as much as it did me. As my aircraft flicked over on its side before going into a vertical dive I saw the Messerschmitt falter and then decide to follow my example. This proved fatal for him.

Just as my nose assumed its vertically downwards position I

was presented with a point blank target of the 109 no more than twenty feet away. Even I could not miss such a heaven presented target. A short burst from my Brownings was sufficient to send him into an inverted spin from which he never recovered. I watched the German aircraft hit the ground in an open field near a wood. Immediately it burst into flames.

By this time sweat was pouring down my face. As it ran into my eyes they smarted painfully. Calling up Micky I was pleased to hear that he, too, had had a successful encounter with a 109. Judging by the general hubbub on the radio I gathered that we had given our visitors a pretty good trouncing. Those Germans who had not been shot down were already winging their way back towards France.

The job was as good as over—for the moment at least. I called up all 'Villa' aircraft and ordered them back to base as soon as possible.

Back on the ground again I felt that in this action I had been able to go some way in coming to grips with my inaccurate shooting. In my own mind, at least, I had vindicated myself after my earlier dreadful attempts at marksmanship in the air.

8 Rudolf Hess talks peace

When a Defiant took off from Prestwick to engage a lone fast-flying aircraft, it had already outpaced a number of Hurricanes which were attempting to intercept it. But shortly after the Defiant got airborne the mystery pilot turned his swift-flying aircraft over on its back and baled out. As he floated down to earth no one had any idea that the man hanging awkwardly below the billowing parachute was Rudolf Hess, second in command to Hitler.

As the Deputy Führer crashed on to British soil, falling badly and breaking an ankle, the commanding officer of R.A.F. Turnhouse, Wing Commander the Duke of Hamilton, was in the station Operations Room keeping in touch with the general situation.

It was Saturday, May 10, 1941, and I was enjoying myself at a small party in Glasgow prior to setting our for Turnhouse to where I had been posted from 602 Squadron. I was to become a fighter controller there two days later and was looking forward to this new role despite the fact that it meant saying 'goodbye' to the squadron with which I had virtually grown up during my early flying life. Although it meant the parting of the ways for us, I was happy that I should be serving again under the Duke of Hamilton, who until the death of his father, to whose title he had succeeded, had been the Marquis of Clydesdale and commanding officer when I started with 602 Squadron.

I already knew Douglo well and, although he was obviously much engaged with the immediate events of Hess's unexpected arrival in Britain when I reached Turnhouse, I was able to glean a little of what was going on and later, of course, he talked about it to me on numerous occasions.

It is a fascinating story but, unfortunately, a great deal of rubbish has been written about it in past years. The Duke of Hamilton is a modest, retiring man who has never sought publicity and has always refrained from talking publicly about the major part he played in what is, undoubtedly, a most historic event. I am therefore honoured that he has allowed me to quote from a verbatim account of what happened on that fateful evening of May 10. It is taken from notes he made at the time.

'I was in the Operations Room when a lone bandit appeared on the Filter Board out to sea at approximately 22.00 hours, flying west at a height of, I think, eighteen thousand feet. The enemy aircraft's track appeared to have crossed the coast near Bamburgh, just south of the Farne Islands and south of the Turnhouse sector.

'I think probably Spitfires at Drem were brought to readiness, but it was a section of Hurricanes from Acklington or Bulmer which were despatched to intercept, and went very wide of the mark. The aircraft, before reaching the coast, was losing height and its speed went up probably to over 300 miles per hour.

'When over the land it flew at low altitude and various Observer Corps observation posts evidently clearly identified it as a ME 110 despite the hoots of derision that greeted this identification in the Operations Room, for an ME 110 was a twin fighter without the endurance to make the return journey to Germany. It certainly does credit to the Observer Corps that, despite this scepticism, which was quickly communicated to them, they firmly stuck to their guns.

'The enemy aircraft flew west at a very low altitude, crossing Scotland and, on account of this, for a short time was lost until it reappeared, having climbed again to about four thousand feet, over the county of Ayr, not far from Dungavel. A Defiant was scrambled from Prestwick and appeared hot on the trail as the ME 110 was milling round, south of Glasgow, possibly trying to find the Dungavel landing ground.

'As this was virtually on the side of a hill, and although all right for light aircraft and gliding, it was quite unsuitable to accommodate a ME 110, especially attempting to land at night, even although, at that time of year, the nights in Scotland are not pitch black.

'At 23.07 hours, news was received in the Operations Room that the enemy aircraft had crashed in flames and we thought that the Defiant had shot it down, but later we were disappointed. Almost at the same time a report was received that a big blitz had started in London. It was therefore unlikely that the Turnhouse sector would be troubled by any more enemy action that night.

'During the previous few nights we had been bothered with scattered enemy aircraft raids of single aircraft flying over Scotland, which had kept the Turnhouse sector active for most of these nights. Now, after this solitary aircraft had been disposed of, everything seemed calm and I went straight to bed and went to sleep; to be almost immediately interrupted by the telephone.

'The Controller's voice demanded that I should return to the Operations Room immediately. I thought that another enemy raid had started; he said he could not divulge the reason, but that I must come at once.

'With the greatest reluctance I crawled out of bed, dressed, and went round to the Operations Room where I was confronted with the news that the pilot of the ME 110 had asked to see me personally, by name, and had given his name as Oberleutnant Alfred Horn.

'During the Olympic Games in 1936 I had seen something of the German Air Force and had noted the names of various German Air Force officers whom I had met. I went through this list and Horn's name did not appear. Information then came through that the German pilot had cracked a bone in his leg on landing by parachute and had been taken to the hospital quarters at Maryhill Barracks.

'I therefore made arrangements to leave for Glasgow early on the 11th with the Intelligence Officer whose duty it was to interrogate the German pilot.

'On arrival at Maryhill Barracks I was first shown the various effects belonging to the German, amongst which were a number of small bottles containing what looked like medicine of different varieties. They were kept away from him. He also had a number of photographs of himself from which I could not recognize him.

'With the Interrogation Officer and the Guard Officer I went into the room where the German was in bed. I do not think I had ever set eyes on him before. When he realized who I was he asked to speak to me alone, and the other two officers withdrew.

'He then told me that he was Rudolf Hess which at first I found difficult to believe, and he started to lay out peace proposals in broken English. I soon withdrew, telling him that an interpreter was required.

'I then telephoned my A.O.C., Air Vice-Marshal Andrews, and told him there was a matter which I could not divulge over the telephone, but which should be reported as soon as possible to the Foreign Office. The A.O.C. was splendid; he asked no questions except who would be in command of the sector during my absence. I borrowed a Hurricane fighter from one of the operational squadrons and flew to Northolt, where I received a message from Mr. Winston Churchill, the Prime Minister, to proceed to Kidlington immediately.

'Unfortunately, an unforeseen delay occurred. An airman, in his enthusiasm to restart the engine quickly for me, liberally overdoped the Merlin engine which then refused to start at all. I could not wait. In my anxiety I ordered the Duty Officer to provide me with another aeroplane. A Magister was then somewhat reluctantly produced for me in which I completed the last lap of my journey to Kidlington.

'A car was waiting and I was taken straight to Ditchley where I reported the matter at first hand to the Prime Minister, who was in remarkably good form despite the fact that the House of Commons had gone up in flames the previous night.

'The next day I flew north in another aeroplane with Ivone Kirkpatrick, who was the German expert at the Foreign Office.

We were met at Turnhouse by Sandy Johnstone. It was Kirkpatrick who formally identified the prisoner as Rudolf Hess.

'During the next few days, because of many commitments, I found I was not in a position to cope with the aeroplanes* I had left scattered around the country.'

In this fashion the Duke was unwittingly drawn into the major affairs of his country somewhat above the level of that normally indulged in by a Wing Commander who is a Station Commander in the Royal Air Force. Granted, he was at that time Lord Steward of the King's Household who on State ceremonial occasions plays a leading role, but is totally non-political. The incident revealed a remarkable ignorance by the leading Nazi officers as to the part played by the Court in relation to the Government of the country.

It revealed, too, how little they realized about our determination to resist the aggression to the bitter end, because the peace proposals outlined by Hess to the Duke of Hamilton were clearly unacceptable to a proud nation serving under such a staunch leader as our war-time Prime Minister. Not surprisingly, the answer, if it had ever been sent back, would have been an uncompromising No.

Rudolf Hess fretted in hospital confinement in Buchanan Castle where he had been removed from Maryhill Barracks on May 12. He fully expected to be treated as a bona fide peace emissary from the Nazi Government. His original intention had been to land his ME 110 at Dungavel, where the Duke of Hamilton had a private landing strip, obtain a satisfactory reply and return to Berlin, his aircraft duly refuelled—no doubt at the British taxpayers' expense.

When he was informed that no such thing was to happen and that he was being kept in Britain as a straightforward prisoner-of-war, he was furious and went almost berserk with

---

* The Hurricane, which belonged to No. 213 Squadron, was later traced to Northolt. It was flown back to Turnhouse where it was commandeered by the Communications Squadron—No. 213 Squadron having by this time left Britain to join the Western Desert Air Force in Egypt.

rage. As time passed and the realization of where his action had led him began to sink into his brain he became extremely eccentric.

And what of Hess today? As Churchill wrote in his *History of the Second World War—Volume III—The Grand Alliance*: 'Reflecting upon the whole of this story, I am glad not to be responsible for the way in which Hess has been and is being treated. Whatever may be the moral guilt of a German who stood near to Hitler, Hess had, in my view, atoned for this by his completely devoted and frantic deed of lunatic benevolence. He came to us of his own free will and, though without authority, had something of the quality of an envoy. He was a medical and not a criminal case and should be so regarded.'

I am in complete agreement with these sentiments. For many years now Hess could surely not be considered a serious menace to anyone. Any crimes he committed have surely been expiated long ago. He is now the only prisoner in Spandau Jail and his continued incarceration there is purely political because the Russians want to maintain their footing in West Berlin. This provides them with such an opportunity.

Repeated pleas to have Hess released have been made by a number of people in recent years. Several influential voices have been heard, but to no great effect. I add my voice to these appeals if only for the reason that there must come a time when mercy must be shown to even the worst of one's enemies. Hess is now a broken man, both in mind and body; few honest people would object if the hand of justice that dealt with him at Nuremberg was now tempered with mercy so that in old age and ill-health he can be cared for by his wife.

9 'Polo ponies may be taken . . .'

While stationed at Turnhouse, Margaret and I set up house in Edinburgh. This was our first proper attempt at family life together and we found it unusual to be able to see so much of each other, something which had not always been possible due to my flying commitments with 602 Squadron. We now had a healthy baby daughter to look after—Ann having been born on April 20.

Apart from such errors as cooking sago in mistake for porridge at breakfast and several disasters with other culinary experiments, our first three months in the Scottish capital were most enjoyable. It was then that my new-found domesticity was shattered when a posting notice came through ordering me to the Middle East to undertake controller duties.

There then began a feverish round of farewells, packing and shopping in an attempt to get me properly kitted out for my sojourn in a warmer climate. Air Ministry sent along a vast array of printed instructions about times, assembly points, label markings and the like. They even went to the trouble of including a pamphlet entitled, 'Hints for officers proceeding overseas for the first time'. Considering we had already been at war for nearly two years some of their so-called hints came as a bit of an eye-opener.

I was informed that each officer was allowed to take with him up to ten cwt. of baggage and that this, whenever possible, was to be packed in wardrobe trunks. It was essential, stressed the pamphlet, that evening clothes were included in the outfit as well as the uniform mess kit.

Polo ponies could normally be obtained less expensively at the intended station of service than at home but, and here the booklet was most explicit and accommodating, arrangements could be made to ship out the officers' own mounts. If a private car was to be taken, a number of licences would be required and these were listed in great detail. The final piece of advice really made my mind boggle because the size of the type on the pamphlet was such that it was obvious Air Ministry laid great stress on the instruction being adhered to—'A licence to carry any sort of firearms must be obtained before these are taken abroad.'

For a moment I was sure that someone, somewhere, must be perpetrating some sort of joke until I turned over and, in tiny type at the foot of the back cover, read: 'Printed May, 1935.'

The voyage to Suez aboard the ex-Royal Mail liner *Almanzora* was something I will always remember. Days and seemingly endless nights in stormy seas round the north of Iceland and far out into the North Atlantic with almost forty merchant ships ploughing through the flying spume and the sight of the majestic aircraft carrier *Argus* 'taking it green' straight over her flight deck while the weather grew increasingly colder as day succeeded day. Then the sudden rise in the temperature as we neared the Azores and our first sight of land as we anchored off Freetown. Rounding the Cape of Good Hope we steered a northwards course up the eastern shores of the African continent until we rendezvoused with H.M.S. *Repulse* before reaching Durban. There were happy times and there were sad times and perhaps upon reflection the most vivid, and certainly the most poignant, was my final sight of the *Repulse* as she took her leave of us as chief escorting ship.

We parted company near Cape Guardafui, at the entrance to the Gulf of Aden. Before she pulled away she steamed at full speed up and down the lines of the convoy. She was fully bedecked and her Marines Corps band played martial airs on the quarterdeck. It was a complimentary gesture which brought a lump to one's throat through sheer pride in one's own comrades in arms. Beneath a cloudless sky and sweltering in the

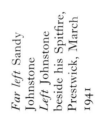

Far left Sandy Johnstone
Left Johnstone beside his Spitfire, Prestwick, March 1941

Opposite above The Avro 504N in which Johnstone learned to fly
Opposite below Hawker Harts of 'C' Flight 602 Squadron,
December 1934
This page above Crash landing by an American B.24 bomber at R.A.F.
Fairwood Common near Swansea
This page below The wreckage of a Halifax bomber which crashed
into the W.A.A.F. site at R.A.F. Fairwood Common

Opposite above The wreckage of Rudolf Hess's ME 110 near Glasgow

Opposite below Bentley Priory, Stanmore, Middlesex, the headquarters of Fighter Command during the Second World War

This page above Geoffrey de Havilland in 1947 at the controls of an experimental aircraft in which he was later killed

This page below Meteor night fighters of 29 Squadron

Opposite above (*l. to r.*) Kevin Fitzgerald and Admiral Lord Mountevans with Sandy Johnstone
Opposite below Johnstone (in dark glasses) with Aidan Crawley, Under-Secretary of State for Air, during an exercise in the Malayan jungle in 1950
This page above Battle of Britain reunion at Biggin Hill, 1955: (*l. to r.*) Air Chief Marshal Lord Dowding, Archie Boyd, Johnstone and Douglas Bader
This page below left Johnstone with Tengku Abdul Rahman at Port Swettenham, July, 1957
This page below right Johnstone with the Duke of Edinburgh and General Peter Hunt at Labuan, Borneo, March, 1965

Above A Gloster Javelin of 33 Squadron prepares for take-off at
R.A.F. Middleton St. George
Below A Shackleton lands at R.A.F. Kinloss in Moray after a long
Atlantic patrol

overpowering heat we listened to the strains of the music drifting towards us then cheered and cheered our farewell greeting to the smartly dressed ship's company drawn up on deck.

Her farewells over, the *Repulse* turned away and took up her station with several ships bound for India. No one would ever see her in Middle East waters again. Several months later, on December 10, in company with the *Prince of Wales*, she was sunk by the Japanese off the coast of Malaya.

At Port Taufiq I said goodbye to the *Almanzora* and in common with the rest of the R.A.F. contingent found myself on the quayside without orders, instructions or even kindly advice. On rooting around I discovered a reasonably intelligent R.A.F. officer who appeared as though 'he might have something to do with it'. He was most apologetic. He agreed that he should 'have had something to do with it' but unfortunately as he had not received any instructions, or even notice of our intended arrival, there was not a great deal he could do right away.

However, he was able to get things moving to a certain extent and eventually buses and lorries arrived to transport us about forty miles up the bank of the Suez Canal to Kasfareet where there was an R.A.F. reception camp. There we were bedded down in tents for the night and I got my first real taste of how cold Egypt could become when the sun dipped swiftly beneath the horizon and darkness fell.

The following morning the Group Captain in charge of postings told me I was destined for Beirut in the Lebanon to help in the establishment of an air defensive organization in the Levant. The R.A.F. Headquarters Levant were in Jerusalem and en route to Beirut I stayed there for two days, meeting the Air Officer Commanding and other members of his staff with whom I would work.

A staff car was put at my disposal and I set off for Beirut by way of Nablus and Haifa. After crossing the border into Syria the road ran parallel with the coast and although the view was pleasant the shocking condition of the roadway did not give me many opportunities to sit back and enjoy my surroundings in

D

comfort. Running northwards through Tyre and Sidon, the Tyre and Sidon of Biblical fame, there were many signs of the damage caused by the recent Naval bombardment. Approaching Beirut the road wound its way through dense pine woods, with row upon row of tall, slender trees standing like an army of silent sentinels, guarding the approaches to the town.

At No. 263 Wing Headquarters, a purple-hued modern house called La Maison sur la Dune which had, until four weeks previously, been the headquarters of General Dentz, the Vichy French military commander, until he was vanquished by British forces, I went in search of Wing Commander Dudley Lewis, the officer commanding the Wing.

I found him in his office, looking extremely pale and suffering from shock. Before I had time to tell him who I was he caught hold of my arm and pointed out of his window.

'Take a look at what that bloody fool has done!' he shouted. I peered out. Almost directly beneath the window lay the tangled wreckage of a small Free French Air Force biplane, smoke and flames still belching from the twisted fuselage. A party of airmen were dragging a badly maimed body clear of the scene of the crash. It was the pilot and judging from the state of his aircraft he must have died on impact.

When Dudley had recovered sufficiently from the shock of the near-miss on his office he told me that the luckless pilot had rashly ignored all previous warnings about low flying and beating up buildings. Shortly before I had arrived the biplane had taken off and the pilot had started to give a display of his prowess as an aviator. His last dive had carried him past Dudley's window with only several feet to spare. At the last moment the Frenchman had found it impossible to pull out. Seconds later he plunged into the large courtyard and the biplane exploded.

Next morning, after a comfortable night in the Normandie Hotel, I got down to work as Squadron Leader Operations. The Fighter operations room was being established in the cellar of the H.Q. building, but it lacked many of the refinements which I had been used to in similar organizations in the U.K.

The information on aircraft movements which we were receiving was sketchy and far from sufficient. Only one small radio location station had been set up to provide early warning of approaching raiders and this only 'read' out to sea as the seven thousand foot mountain to the east of Beirut completely blanketed the inland area from the searching pulses of the R.D.F. set.

'Doggie' Searl and Tommy Thomson, the latter an early wartime acquaintance of mine who had been a controller at Turnhouse, had been in Beirut since the town had been captured and had already worked wonders in getting things started. Doggie, in particular, was one of those bright and cheery chaps who are always bubbling over with enthusiasm. He had immediately appreciated the grave shortcomings of the radio location equipment in not being able to tell us anything about what was going on in the air overland and had most effectively made his number with the local Chef de Police.

The result was that he had managed to organize the Lebanese gendarmerie into a passable imitation of the Observer Corps. Unfortunately these worthy fellows could not speak English, making it necessary to employ a couple of 'filterers' who could translate from the French or Arabic as the case might be. The 'filterers' sat in a small room, next door to the Operations Room, as security rulings debarred us from permitting them to enter this holy of holies. A junior R.A.F. officer was normally stationed with them to ensure that they did not fall asleep or otherwise get up to any mischief.

One of the biggest headaches we had to contend with was the blackout. The delightful Lebanese people were completely hopeless when it came to trying to insist that *all* traces of light should be obscured from outside at night. The best they could manage was to make Beirut look for all the world like a Chinese fairground in full swing. Eventually when the situation grew more hopeless and dangerous we were forced to take a firm hand and approach the Mayor. He was most co-operative, but pointed out, quite reasonably, that it was not in his people's nature to take a thing like war at all seriously. Furthermore, he emphasized, he did not think that any amount of threatening or cajoling would do the slightest bit of good.

This situation placed us in a bit of a dilemma. We had no wish to antagonize the local people who, in the main, behaved with a great deal of charm, going about their everyday business with a deliberate air of cheerfulness. The relationship between them and their new invaders, the British, was, on the whole, a good one. However, it was important that steps were taken to remedy the blackout problem, otherwise disaster was likely to strike, swiftly and surely, and involve everyone, British and Lebanese alike.

We reached the conclusion that the only effective way to deal with the matter was to arrange a system of warnings with the electricity power house people themselves and to get them to pull out the plug on the approach of hostile aircraft. The main drawback was, of course, that all electricity would be cut off at the power station. This was certain to cause a series of problems.

All the same, we agreed it was much better to endure some minor hardships than provide a brilliantly illuminated target on which enemy aircraft could drop bombs at will.

This scheme worked perfectly when put into practice on trial runs. After giving the electrical chaps a few practice 'Alertes Jaunes' and 'Alertes Rouges' we were satisfied that an adequate blackout would be maintained in case of need.

A few weeks later the Deputy Chief of the Air Staff, Air Marshal Sir Douglas Evill, made a tour of inspection in the Middle East and arrived in Beirut with the rest of his party. After lunch in the mess we all gathered in the small cellar-like operations room in La Maison sur la Dune. While Sir Douglas was having the lay-out of the operations network explained to him an enemy aircraft's plot appeared suddenly on the board.

'This is grand,' I thought. 'What a chance to show the Old Man how efficient we are in 263 Wing.'

Scrambling a section of Hurricanes from Haifa, a job which took about ten minutes because there was still no direct telephone line to that sector, the 'Alerte Jaune' was passed to the local A.R.P. organization. Because the weather was perfect, with little cloud and bright sunshine, we felt confident there was every hope of carrying out an interception.

Within seconds of the alert being passed on, the operations room was plunged into darkness. Not even the smallest pinprick of light managed to penetrate the gloom of the cellar. I shouted to the Ops Room corporal to light the twelve hurricane lamps which I personally had checked to ensure they had sufficient paraffin. The corporal leapt into action and struck match after match but no light came from the lamps. Silence hung over the room—it seemed pointless to speak. There was considerable speculation in my mind as to what Sir Douglas and his party were thinking of what was going on around them. Had we been able to see the poor corporal's face I'm sure he must have been blushing violently as he fumbled at the feet of the Air Marshal, scratching matches without any success.

The Duty Controller started to add to the confusion by floundering around looking for a telephone. He felt he should at least call someone to tell of our predicament. Pencils and logbooks fell on to the floor as his hands roamed over the tables. Every so often the Ops Room orderly was despatched outside to see and report on the latest position of the German reconnaissance aircraft, which was now almost directly overhead. On his return he, too, struck matches and placing his finger on the appropriate position on the plotting board tried to hold it in position long enough for the controller to get a bearing before the spluttering match burned his fingers.

Sir Douglas and his party grew restless and for want of something to do to relieve the monotony moved forward to catch a glimpse of the aircraft's plot themselves. Several officers stumbled over the edge of the controller's dais, sending several trays of plotting counters and other accessories tumbling on to the floor. There was more confusion when, realizing what they had done, they side-stepped to avoid standing on the objects on the floor and bumped into each other, starting considerable jostling for position throughout the entire assembly.

I did not need to see any faces to know that the tension making itself felt through the gloom meant that tempers were rapidly approaching flash-point. Slipping out of the room as unobtrusively as I could I went upstairs to find out what had gone wrong with the lights.

Then—and only then—did the answer dawn on me. Our faithful Beirut Electricity Department had taken us absolutely at our word and, in spite of its being brilliant daylight, had cut off the power as soon as the alert had been given.

Leaving instructions that the power station was to be contacted with instructions to restore the electricity I hurried downstairs to inform the others of what had happened. I had barely entered the room (where, to my silent amusement, there were now several matches in full flame, but still no gleam from the hurricane lamps), when the lights came on again. Before anyone had time to readjust their eyes to the sudden brightness, I helped to hustle them outside and up the stairs as quickly as possible.

Once they were out of the way I took a close look at the traitorous hurricane lamps. They were filled to the brim with the necessary lamp oil, as I had thought—but not one of them boasted a wick.

Surprisingly Sir Douglas did not dwell on the chaos of the operations room and the incident, although talked about and laughed over in private, was soon forgotten officially. Nevertheless, I often wondered why we were not all posted after allowing such a show of inefficiency to take place in the presence of such distinguished company.

It began to snow in Beirut—a rare occurrence indeed. I was told that the last time there had been so much snow in the town had been twenty-three years previously when British troops had last been stationed in the Lebanon. I'm glad, however, that the superstitious among the natives did not lay the blame at our door. So great was the snowfall that, for nearly a week, snowploughs made regular appearances in the main streets. At first I was puzzled as to why the civic authorities should keep large machines such as snowploughs in a town which is renowned for its warm climate. I realized later, of course, that the Cedars of Lebanon, one of the best ski-ing centres in the world, was only about thirty-five miles away. In fact the Cedars itself had received so much snow that the inhabitants were forced to temporarily evacuate the place, put on their skis, and slide all the way down to Tripoli.

As our operations room set-up developed we built a separate radio transmitting station on a piece of waste land about sixty yards from the main headquarters building. Telephone wires were laid across the ground to connect this new building with the main block. A few days after this layout was completed the wireless sergeant informed me that a length of telephone wire was missing. On rigging up a fresh wire we discovered that this vanished too, having been stolen during the night.

The next consignment of wire was strung up on telegraph poles but, in spite of this, the usual section, ten yards of cable, was duly reported as having vanished, cut with wire cutters.

The damaged wire was replaced and a watch kept when darkness fell. It was not long before the culprit was caught in the act of snipping off a piece of wire. He was a scruffy-looking Arab, with very little English and even less money, judging by his unkempt appearance. After his capture he kept wringing his hands and bewailing that he had only taken the wire to tie up bundles of merchandise on to the back of his donkey.

Jackaman, our Signals Officer, decided that the time was ripe to have a warning notice painted and nailed to one of the poles. Its message was simple: 'Anyone approaching within ten yards of this notice will be shot on sight.'

The text was written in English, Arabic, French, Yiddish and even Greek. Proudly, Jacko surveyed his handiwork and sent some men to place it in position. There was only one snag to the sign—it had been written in so many languages that the writing turned out to be extremely small; so small, in fact, that one had to approach the sign and go right up to it in order to read what was written. However, after firing off a few rounds well over the heads of the would-be wire snatchers, the telephone link was left alone and we were allowed to get on with our operations with considerably fewer interruptions.

Dudley Lewis left us in the middle of January, 1942, and our new commanding officer was Victor Croome, a hearty Croup Captain, who, when he laughed, and that was often, made a noise like the gushing of a soda siphon. Like Dudley he became extremely popular with everyone.

I was able to keep my hand in at flying all the time I was with 263 Wing as we had a small two-seater Magister, kept as a communications aircraft. Victor and I were the only two officers there who were fully qualified pilots so there was never any problem in getting a hold of the aircraft when we felt like a flight.

In the hangars at Beirut Airport we found an undamaged Cant three-engined bomber which the Italians had left behind during their retreat at the outbreak of hostilities in the Lebanon. Victor and I cast covetous glances at this large aircraft and very quickly set the wheels in motion to have it officially taken over as a legitimate prize of war. Two of the three engines were unserviceable, however, and the chief snag lay in acquiring suitable replacements.

Victor and I were not the only ones interested in the bomber and when we discovered this it was too late to do anything about it. The Free French Air Force were too quick for us. Somehow or other they managed to get hold of two American engines which they succeeded in bending into shape in order to have them fixed to the Cant. Once they had done this they put in a counter-claim on the grounds that they had made the bomber serviceable again. They won the day and after painting large Croix de Lorraine all over the wings and fuselage prepared to fly it over to their headquarters airfield at Damascus.

Sadly, Victor and I watched our prize slipping through our fingers but, as the bomber took off, we derived some satisfaction from the unearthly din being made by the engines.

Whether the cause of the trouble was the original engine or its two American neighbours we did not know, but as it climbed away and became a speck above the hills we were still able to hear traces of the peculiar noise.

Both Victor and I must have had rather mean minds in those days. We were quite consoled when we heard later that the pilot of the Cant had messed up his approach to Damascus and ended up by crashing as he touched down on the runway. No one had been badly hurt but we rubbed our hands when told that the bomber, on this occasion, was most definitely not repairable.

Beirut in spring is a sight worth seeing. Great masses of exotic flowers burst into life and fill the air with a glorious aroma. Everywhere the streets are lined with trees weighed down by their cloaks of blossom. It is a time when the town becomes alive with colour and the very nature of the surroundings are such that they quickly affect one's personality until even the most depressed is given a new outlook on life. For us, stationed there at a difficult stage in the war, the beauty of the town was a welcome boost to our morale although everyone knew that the idyllic period would be over all too quickly, providing no more than a fleeting prelude of several weeks to the long, dry summer with its months of heat and sticky humidity.

For me there was to be no summer in Beirut. In March my promotion to Wing Commander came through and I knew I would soon have to leave because the established rank for my job was that of Squadron Leader. Late in April it was again time to pack my bags and set off for Palestine to take command of the Sector Headquarters at Haifa.

My predecessor at Haifa was an Australian, Wing Commander 'Digger' Black. Like nearly all Australians he acquired the nickname of 'Digger' and not once did I ever hear him being mentioned by his proper Christian name—whatever that may have been. He had already achieved a considerable reputation for himself in the R.A.F. and indeed throughout all circles in the Middle East. As officer commanding the R.A.F. in Tobruk he had been a tower of strength and inspiration to everyone during a difficult and dangerous time. Taking over from someone of this calibre was certainly no sinecure and I still had a couple of months to go before I reached my twenty-sixth birthday.

The R.A.F. headquarters was situated in a charming house in the French Carmel district with the operations block in a large building standing on the edge of a cliff, providing a commanding all-round view of Haifa, the surrounding countryside and the Mediterranean Sea. Considering the role it was expected to play it had been built in one of the most conspicuous sites available for miles around. Even a U-boat could have surfaced some miles off the coast and knocked it for six.

Fortunately one never did go so far as to fire a shell at us, although on one occasion an underwater raider popped up its conning tower only two miles from the shore where it was spotted almost at once and rendered immobile by the good marksmanship of a Naval destroyer. Anxious to capture the prize intact, in order to probe it for any new developments, the destroyer started to close in.

There was not much distance left between the British vessel and the German when the coastal batteries opened up with all the force they could muster. The submarine was hit directly amidships and within seconds there was nothing left of her except an oil slick on the water and floating pieces of debris.

I heard later that the men who manned the shore guns had been waiting for such an opportunity to present itself since the outbreak of the war and as someone said: 'We were damned if we were going to let a chance like that slip from under our noses.'

This was the only occasion on which these guns went into action throughout the entire war. Perhaps the spirits of those who manned them were dampened too much by the inevitable barrage of disapproval which descended on them as a result of sinking the U-boat from beneath the destroyer's nose. Whatever anyone felt officially about their action all were agreed that it had been a rattling good shot.

The railway line which ran across the Sinai Desert, connecting Palestine with Egypt, terminated at Haifa and it was not until 1942 that the work of extending it northwards as far as Beirut was seriously put in hand. A South African Engineer battalion undertook the job and in an incredibly short space of time blasted and dug its way through the seventy-mile route along the coast. One of the first trains to run on the new stretch was a 'special' carrying the nursing staff of an Australian hospital being transferred from Beirut.

No wayside stations had been built, so a stop was arranged en route for the convenience of the travellers. This was to be at a deserted spot somewhere north of Tyre. Unhappily, the engine broke down several miles from the official halting place and the nurses, fully anticipating a stop around this area, got out to stretch their legs. The engine driver was much too busy attending to the peculiarities of his locomotive to notice the exodus of his passengers. The fault was located, quickly repaired and off went the train, minus most of the nurses. Fortunately the driver of a passing car spotted the women gathered together and gesticulating in the direction taken by the train. They told him of their predicament and he raced ahead managing eventually, after some fast driving, to make the engine driver pull up.

Two days later another train broke down at almost the same spot and on this occasion it was the engine driver's turn to stop a passing car to ask the driver if he would give him a lift to Haifa so that he could get replacement parts for his locomotive. That particular journey took the train almost twenty-four hours to complete—hardly a record for seventy miles.

The longer I spent at Haifa the more worried I became about the vulnerable position of the Stella Maris section operations room. I approached Colonel Bonn, the officer commanding the Royal Engineers in Haifa, to see whether he could offer any alternative suggestions for resiting.

Surveying the possible safer places where we might reconstruct the outfit without interfering too much with the existing complicated telephone network, we decided that the most suitable alternative was to erect an entirely new reinforced concrete building in a disused quarry about four hundred yards from the existing site. Plans were drawn up and sent to headquarters for approval.

For some time we waited for news of our suggestions, but every enquiry was met with the stock reply that the matter was still under consideration. As the wheels of officialdom seemed to be grinding exceedingly slowly Colonel Bonn decided to take a chance and go ahead with our project on the assumption that the scheme would meet with ultimate approval. Hundreds of Royal Engineers and civilian labourers were despatched to the quarry and set up a collection of sighting poles, wooden huts and concrete mixers.

Rapidly, a gigantic concrete building started to take shape and it soon became obvious that it was large enough to house three operations rooms in addition to dozens of offices and a canteen to service the affair. The larger it grew the more apprehensive I became about its reception when headquarters got to hear about it. I expressed my fears to the colonel on several occasions but the only consolation I could get from this quarter was a hearty: 'Don't worry, old boy—we might as well be hung for a sheep as a lamb.'

When the building was finally erected and all the necessary sanitary facilities added we stepped back to see the finished article. I was horrified by its size although I was forced to admit to the satisfied colonel that it did look an impressive affair. However, it also looked extremely conspicuous, despite our original intentions and I flew Colonel Bonn over the area so that he could see for himself. Nothing daunted, the gallant colonel arrived at the site on the following day with several soldiers carrying bundles of dynamite. For several seconds I thought he had taken leave of his senses.

'Good heavens, Colonel,' I enquired in horror, 'you're not going to blow it up, are you?'

He considered my suggestion to be a huge joke, but even after he had finished laughing he still would not tell me what he intended to do.

'Patience, old boy, patience. Just you wait and see.'

I climbed back into my car and fled from the site, not trusting my eyes to witness anything else the colonel might decide to do. I had barely settled down in my office when several loud explosions, followed by a dull rumbling, rather like distant thunder, announced that, whatever it was, the worst had happened. Donning my cap I jumped back into my car and raced down the hill to the quarry. Clouds of thick dust hung in the air all around the place and to my amazement I saw that the quarry had altered appreciably in shape. Colonel Bonn had blasted away its sides and had succeeded in pulling most of the rubble over the top of the new Operations block giving it all the camouflage it required and making it extremely difficult to pick out from the air.

Although the finished product was now satisfactory from my point of view approval had still not been given for its construction, and to make my feelings of apprehension even more intense, word came through that the Commander-in-Chief, Air Chief Marshal Sir Arthur Tedder, would be visiting Haifa to carry out a routine inspection.

He was due to arrive by air at St. Jean and 'Digger' Black, who was now a Group Captain instructor at the Middle East Staff School across the waadi from our headquarters, and I went up to meet him. Some days previously 'Digger' had met the Army Provost Marshal and had mentioned, casually, that the C.-in-C. was coming to Haifa. The Provost Marshal immediately made arrangements to have several military outriders on motor cycles to escort the distinguished visitor the sixteen miles from the airfield to our headquarters. When 'Digger' and I arrived we found the R.A.F. Provost Marshal, not to be outdone by his opposite number, had arranged a similar contingent of R.A.F. police outriders. Anxious that they, too, would not be left out of the security network, the Palestine Police had also sent a detachment of motor cyclists to act as escort.

The cavalcade, reminiscent of the sort of bodyguard given to a Head of State, consisting of my staff car with Air Chief Marshal Tedder aboard, preceded by six expert motor cyclists equipped with sirens and followed by numerous others, charged out from the airfield and swept on to the main Haifa-Beirut road.

At times we travelled at well over 60 m.p.h. Approaching traffic quickly pulled on to the verge of the road when they heard the wailing sirens and when we roared past I'm sure they must have been almost choked by the amount of dust thrown up by the pounding wheels. The pace did not slacken much as we negotiated several of the Haifa streets, and even climbing the hill to Mount Carmel was no problem for the fast-moving convoy.

The furious pace at which we were being driven was not conducive to speech and little was said, due to the hair-raising journey, to prepare the Air Chief Marshal for his first view of the new Operations Block. In grand style we braked to a halt outside the quarry and, when everyone had composed themselves, prepared to leave the car. The C.-in-C. stepped out into the sunlight and I watched his face as he gazed at the building. I saw his expression change to what I considered to be a frown. Then he spun round and addressed me.

'What the dickens is this—the Dorchester Hotel?'

Despite his look of astonishment I detected the shadow of a twinkle in his eyes, so I got in with my story of how it had come to be built. Explanations over, the inspection went ahead and the scheme was given official blessing. What a moment of relief that was; for weeks I had lived in dread of being asked to pay for its construction out of my own pocket although, no doubt, Colonel Bonn would have helped me out if the going had become rough. He was a great friend to the R.A.F. in Haifa and a man who believed firmly in getting the job done—then arguing about the details afterwards.

Due to the Air Chief Marshal's exclamatory remark, the Operations Block became known as 'The Dorchester'. The operations telephone exchange even adopted the title and, instead of picking up a telephone and asking the operator for 'Operations 52' or 'Operations 17' or whatever number one wanted, it became the regular custom to ask for 'Dorchester 52' or 'Dorchester 17'. Everyone started to enter into the spirit of the occasion and I suppose, in one way, we initiated our own secret code to help protect the identity of the mammoth building which had been situated in a quarry.

10 *When Malta stood alone*

Dozens of bales of rubber boots, sacks of dehydrated potatoes, one ominous-looking naval torpedo and Major-General Beckett, General Officer Commanding the artillery in Malta, accompanied me in the bomb well of a Liberator as the aircraft made its touch-down at Luqa airfield. It was September, 1942, and I had arrived in the island to take up more flying duties with a Spitfire Wing.

The first person to greet me, a familiar face, was Frank Tyson, at one time the regular adjutant of Edinburgh's Auxiliary 603 Squadron. He was now one of the two Wing Commander deputy station commanders at Luqa.

Next morning I cadged a lift on the ration waggon and went into Valetta, the capital, to report my arrival to headquarters, situated in The Ditch—a long cavern which extended about two hundred feet down into the soft porous rock of the island. Other than by receiving a direct hit it was immune from air-raid damage. To the back of the small concrete offices, which served as the administrative headquarters, the cliff face was honeycombed with subterranean passages hewn out from the centre of the rock. Inside one of these the Operations Room had been constructed.

I was taken to see the A.O.C., Air Vice-Marshal Keith Park, who had also been my A.O.C. in 1940 when I was with 602 Squadron at Westhampnett. It was he who had commanded the Fighter Group which had been mainly responsible for the successful outcome of the Battle of Britain.

As it had taken me nearly two weeks to get from Palestine to

Malta he explained that he had been forced to hand over the Spitfire Wing to another officer pending my arrival. As this fellow was proving his worth, explained Air Vice-Marshal Park, it was only fair that he should be allowed to continue for a time. In the meantime I was to be sent to Luqa, along with Frank Tyson, as the other deputy station commander. This arrangement suited me admirably, particularly as it would not only give me a chance to become acclimatized to siege conditions, but it would also allow me the opportunity of getting my hand in once more at operational techniques before having to lead a Wing into action myself. I felt certain that my know-how must have become rusty after almost two years away from aerial combat.

Bill le May was the Group Captain in command at Luqa, an Auxiliary Air Force officer like myself, who had already been in Malta for many months and whose experience was invaluable in assisting me to become settled in.

Luqa was the only airfield in Malta on which it was possible to land large aircraft. It was, in consequence, most essential to maintain its runways in serviceable order as our only means of sustenance was coming by air at that time. Malta, so recently the recipient of the George Cross, was still licking its wounds after one of the most concentrated and long-drawn-out bombardments in the history of the war.

The people were constantly hungry as no food ships had ventured near the island since the ill-fated August convoy had taken such a beating. Apart from the destruction of supply ships the Royal Navy had lost H.M.S. *Eagle, Manchester, Cairo* and one destroyer.

The air provided our only link and for everyone's sake Luqa had to be kept in as good a state of repair as was possible. Two of the five fighter squadrons were also based there. At one end of the landing ground were the remains of a small stone tower, which, in fact, was the only building left standing. Below this was an exceptionally deep air-raid shelter and the entire set-up was referred to as 'G' shelter. This was where passengers emplaning for overseas flights congregated when the frequent raids by Luftwaffe JU 88's and Stukas interrupted their departure.

On top of 'G' Shelter tower a field telephone had been placed to connect direct with the Operations Room in The Ditch. Frank and I took it in turns to sit on top of this tower to plot the bombs as they fell on the airfield and issue the local air-raid warnings. Immediately the bombing ceased, we would shin down the ladder, jump into our little Ford car, filled with red flags, and drive to place a flag on every bomb crater which pitted the runways. Six or seven lorries loaded with clinker and gravel were always kept standing by to race out after us and to make for the flag-marked holes into which they dumped their loads.

A dilapidated steam roller brought up the rear of this strange caravan and made peculiar noises as it puffed and trundled its way back and forth along the runways. The longest it ever took to put them into a serviceable condition was twenty minutes, which said a great deal for the efficiency of the labour.

On one occasion there had been a particularly large amount of damage done to the runway in use and the army of labourers excelled themselves in shovelling and pressing the gravel into the holes ready for the faithful old road roller to go to work. Feverishly, with tremendous spasms of energy it panted over the roughly filled cavities, two of which were right at the edge of the runway itself.

Standing back to make a final check to ensure that we could call in the waiting fighters, sweeping and circling around high overhead as they waited for the signal, and feeling well satisfied with the job just finished, we headed towards the shelter to await the landings. We had only covered a short distance when a deafening explosion made us all stop short in our tracks. We raced in the direction of the dust cloud and found a large hole, just off the runway, where a delayed action bomb had just gone off. 'Faithful Annie', our steam roller, had escaped miraculously. Only ten minutes before she had been plying backwards and forwards over the spot where this monstrous weapon had been lying.

Malta, at its largest, is only seventeen miles in length and seven miles across. In spite of its small size it was estimated that in 1942 there were well over ten thousand separate farms dotted over the landscape. Their fields, divided by dry-stone dykes, made it impossible for an aircraft to attempt to make a forced landing anywhere except at one of the three airfields— Luqa, Takali or Halfar. Midway between Luqa and Halfar a landing strip, known as Saafi, had been in the course of preparation, but work stopped on the project shortly before I arrived on the island.

Into this had been bundled dozens of wrecked aircraft, both allied and enemy, which had either been shot straight into the ground or had attempted to make forced landings and had smashed their ways through a series of stone walls after hitting the ground. This place was known by everyone as the Grave-yard.

From it, however, all salvable equipment was drawn in order to try to maintain our own aircraft, spare parts being virtually unobtainable otherwise. The only armoured tank in the island, a Crusader, was pressed into service to help remove the remains of the crashed aircraft and for some time there were few idle moments for either tank or crew.

One felt a great sense of loneliness in Malta. No matter how high was the morale at any particular time, when one thought about the isolated position of our fortress it seemed, at times, that the odds against our continuing survival were very great indeed. Axis-held Sicily lay less than seventy miles to the north and, similarly, Tripolitania lay not far to the south. The islands of Lampedusa and Pantellaria lying to the west of Malta were always a constant threat to our peace of mind. Hedged in on all sides by the enemy, who pounded away at our defences with relentless determination, we had to look over twelve hundred miles away to find our nearest friends in either Egypt or Gibraltar.

Lack of foodstuffs and heating were the principal worries to both civilians and military personnel alike. Food stocks were diminishing at an alarming rate and the half part of a small loaf of bread, issued each morning with breakfast, had to suffice for the day and was carried everywhere one went. Now and again a packet of dehydrated potatoes, or vegetables, came to light, but they were difficult to prepare as there was no fuel available for cooking. Wood was at a premium as Malta is not an island which grows many trees.

On occasions a few small eggs were sent across from the neighbouring island of Gozo, but the majority of these rightly found their way into the hospitals. If one succeeded in finding eggs available on the black market the price was never less than 10s. each. At this price one had to make a proper meal of it, lingering over the golden yolk as one might do with a superb steak in a restaurant famed for its cuisine.

The shortage of petrol seriously hampered our operations and the squadrons had to be severely limited in their activities. However severe an air-raid became, squadrons which had used up their day's quota of petrol had to stop flying and disperse on the ground. A sufficient reserve had always to be kept in hand to provide adequate aerial cover for the next convoy when it did come. There was little doubt that the enemy quickly grew to realize our predicament and as a result piled on the pressure as much as they could.

Normal safety standards were waived in drastic fashion and one was not allowed to taxi aircraft except to clear them from the duty runways; nor was it permitted to 'run up' the engines prior to take-off. Engine failures were remarkably few under the circumstances, but they occurred nevertheless more frequently than usual. This shortage of fuel had repercussions, too, in affecting the amount of materials which could be flown into the island, as the aircraft making the journey from Egypt or Gibraltar had to carry sufficient petrol on board to complete the two thousand four hundred mile round trip.

It was impossible to run a private car and the number of motor vehicles to be seen in the island was negligible. The Governor, Lord Gort, was provided with one, as were the Naval, Army and Air Force commanders. Apart from a number of lorries and vans which were essential to the maintenance of supplies the only other cars one saw were used by the operational aircrews who had to have them to get to and from the airfields and their billets.

The Krendi Wing was supplied with a monstrous old Chevrolet with one side of its bodywork entirely missing, and into which twelve pilots would squeeze themselves. With bicycles being the only other means of transport, and after a time even these were at a premium, even the Governor took to using one to go about his business. Considerable difficulty was always experienced when the Chevrolet, packed tight with pilots, met Lord Gort, who was a familiar figure as he cycled along the roads between the various airfields.

What should have been a succession of smart salutes normally developed into something more reminiscent of the waving of arms in good natured greetings on both sides. But no one minded—least of all the Governor.

Everyone had the greatest admiration for Lord Gort and it was no uncommon thing to find both him and his A.D.C. on the airfields before daylight talking to pilots and ground crew as they prepared to take off on the dawn patrol. There is little doubt that his ability to endure the hardships inflicted on everyone in Malta and his intense interest in all manner of problems, whether large or small, made him a popular figure and the ideal man to lead a community which was always virtually under siege.

As time wore on it was decided to evacuate as many civilians as possible. This was not such a huge task as it may appear because the aircraft returning from Malta were carrying only a half load of fuel and no cargo. On one occasion fifty-three people, including the crew, packed themselves into a Dakota. With the normal complement for this type of Dakota being twenty-four many of us felt it highly unlikely that the aircraft would ever be able to lift itself off the ground. Along the runway ran the Dakota, its two sturdy engines straining and heaving to lift the great load. After what seemed to be an age the faithful 'Gooney Bird', as the Americans affectionately dubbed the Dakota because of its ability to do almost anything asked of it, rose slowly into the air. Foot by foot it climbed and turned away carrying what must surely have been a record number of people for any Dakota, on the long flight to Cairo.

Now that food stocks had reached a remarkably low level many supplementary items had to be brought into use to stave off the pangs of hunger. These consisted of a watery type of soup, which had small pieces of grass floating around in it, and occasional stews made from goat's flesh, although at times we were certain that dog meat was being used. The highlight was a sort of pasty dish resembling macaroni which had been flattened out before being cooked. Hot dishes were liberally speckled with large blobs of soot, as the only means of heating the food was over mocked-up stoves, which worked on the principle of dripping burning salvaged engine oil on to a metal plate. The sole flavouring was in the form of large chunks of coarse salt. Taking everything into account our digestive organs must have had a fairly trying time.

Disinfectants were also running out and this became a most serious problem when an epidemic of scabies broke out among the girls who worked in the confined quarters of the under-ground Operations Room. To us, one of the major tragedies of this period was when we had to sacrifice our one and only bottle of whisky for use as a disinfectant for the Ops Room telephone.

Towards the end of November I moved into Valetta to take on the job of a fighter controller in the Operations Room. 'Dusty' Millar was the Group Captain commanding the fighters in the island and Charles Griffiths, Bill Farnes and, later, Roger Frankland were the other controllers.

The plotting table in the Ops Room showed a picture of a small section of the central Mediterranean area with Malta in the centre. The southern half of Sicily also appeared, as did the islands of Lampedusa and Pantellaria—what remained was just sea. We were able to sit and watch the plotted movements of Nazi aircraft while they flew over their bases, as the radar installations in Malta were highly effective.

One day when the weather around Malta was too bad to operate any of our fighters we were surprised when our special wireless intelligence people informed us that an air-raid warning had just been sounded at Comiso in southern Sicily and that the Germans had sent up two squadrons of their fighters to meet a supposed British raid approaching from the south.

As the Intelligence people listened in to all enemy wireless transmissions we were always kept well informed as to what was going on at the other side. The information was normally highly reliable—and useful. No doubt the enemy did the same with our transmissions and as a result we both had to be considerably guarded as to what we said over the radio.

The opportunity that presented itself was too good to miss. I picked up the mouthpiece of the transmitting set and called up one of our squadrons which I knew was securely grounded out at Takali.

'Hello Tommy—hello Tommy—keep a sharp lookout at three o'clock below you,' I shouted. 'Many little jobs are coming up to intercept—repeat many little jobs are coming up to intercept.'

I waited for news of the Germans having intercepted the message. Sure enough, several minutes later, Intelligence reported that they had picked up an order from the German control to their fighters to look out above as the British aircraft would soon be on top of them.

'Hello Tommy—hello Tommy—steer a course of 020 degrees,' was my next instruction to the mythical airborne squadron. Within two minutes the plots of the ME 109's and FW 190's appeared on the table streaking northwards on a course of 020 degrees.

'Hello Tommy—hello Tommy—steer a course of 270 degrees —repeat 270 degrees.'

Westward ho! went the enemy in strict obedience to the command.

We kept up this performance for almost thirty minutes, making the German aircraft go round in circle after circle like a swarm of angry bees as they searched the sky for signs of the phantom squadron. So far did they travel and in such a wide variety of directions that they must have had one of the best conducted tours of Sicily ever laid on for any occasion.

Ordering our fictitious squadron to return to base and issuing instructions for the aircraft to land immediately, we had the satisfaction of watching the German plots disappear one by one as the pilots of the fighters returned bewildered, and we hoped thoroughly exhausted, to their own bases.

The fighters controlled from the Valletta Operations Room were responsible for shooting down well over a thousand enemy aircraft during the first four years of the war—an impressive total indeed—and it was generally a scene of considerable activity at all times of the day and night.

Early in December we received word that a convoy of four merchant ships, escorted by a cruiser and three destroyers, was going to attempt to reach us from Port Said. The news sparked off intense excitement in all quarters of the island and our fighters were prepared for maximum effort to repel the attacks we knew would surely come. Although there was silent jubilation at the good news, it was obvious the Germans and Italians would do all in their power to prevent relief from reaching Malta.

The time dragged past until at last, as the convoy steamed nearer and nearer, our long-range fighters were able to patrol the area and provide an aerial umbrella over their heads. The news that the ships were close spread like wildfire throughout the island and the people congregated in their thousands along the shores of the Grand Harbour, eager for the first sighting of the gallant ships.

Time and again enemy aircraft tried to break through the tight cordon thrown over the area for miles around the convoy, but in a series of savage fights were driven back. Gradually, one by one, they withdrew and at 10 a.m. on a Saturday morning the first of the merchantmen swung slowly into the harbour entrance, followed closely by the three others. Then came the cruiser, immaculately dressed overall, her Marine band playing on the quarterdeck.

The Maltese went mad in a frenzied outburst of tears, laughter and loud unrestrained cheering. Young boys and girls leaped and screamed, while their parents roared themselves hoarse as they watched the long-awaited convoy gliding in to safety. Old and young hugged and kissed each other; a few people just stood quietly, the tears of relief rolling unashamedly down their cheeks. Everywhere there were scenes of delirium and for the men aboard the ships in the convoy it must have been a sight to remember as the people showed their appreciation with such enthusiasm. I have never seen such a heartfelt welcome being given to any force as was given to that small band of mariners who had opened up the sea route once again and given Malta the chance to breathe more easily.

To me it was an added delight because the escorting cruiser was the *Euryalus*, the ship on which I had spent so many enjoyable hours while in Palestine. I wasted no time in hiring a dghaisa to take me out to her and was on board before she had even completed mooring operations.

Many friends on board made me welcome and quickly guessed the reason for my hasty arrival.

I was taken to the wardroom and within minutes was tucking into the first square meal I had seen for months. Stuffing myself with all kinds of good fare I thanked my friends for their kindness and returned to the Ops Room to take over my spell of duty. My colleagues were highly envious of my good fortune and I made the most of the situation by describing to them in great detail the various kinds of food I had eaten. But my gluttony and good-natured gloating got the better of me. Not long after settling down to work fierce stabs of pain gripped my stomach and in next to no time I was forced to go back to my quarters; for the next two days I lay in bed as my digestive organs gradually returned to normal after the beating they had taken.

While aboard the *Euryalus* I had been delighted to hear that our air cover had been so effective that no one aboard had seen a single enemy aircraft on the voyage from Egypt nor, for that matter, had there been any signs of U-boat activity.

The arrival of the convoy was certainly a turning-point in the island's life. From then on small convoys were able to make regular trips without being molested unduly and one of the main effects of this new lease of life was that we could think again in terms of offensive operations instead of always being on the defensive. To help matters both the Germans and Italians eased off their operations and gave us a chance to conserve the fuel and ammunition stocks which had been replenished, thanks to the convoy.

In January, 1943, I was given command of one of the three Spitfire Wings—my one comprising of Nos. 229 and 249 Squadrons based on the newly built air strip at Krendi.

No. 229 Squadron had had an interesting career as it had arrived in Malta as 603 Squadron—my old friends from Edinburgh—after having flown off an aircraft carrier midway between Gibraltar and Malta. It had been their intention to make only a transit stop in the island for refuelling purposes before proceeding to the Western Desert where the ground crews of the unit, having travelled out by sea, were already waiting for their aircraft to turn up.

Intensive operations were taking place in Malta when they touched down and it was decided that the sixteen Spitfires would serve a more useful purpose on the island than in the Western Desert, so they were retained. Consequently, it was found there were two 603 Squadrons—one in Malta with aircraft, but no ground crews, and one in Egypt with ground crews, but no aircraft. As the majority of the ground crew personnel still retained their Auxiliary status it was decided, quite rightly, to allow them to retain the original squadron number and to allocate another number to the flying part of it which had long since lost the services of its Auxiliary Air Force members.

Krendi was a strange landing ground. A runway had been constructed hard alongside the edge of a cliff, so much so that at one time we seriously considered putting up safety nets in much the same way as they are strung up over the sides of aircraft carriers. However, this idea was shelved when we found that the aircraft were not showing any undue tendencies to swing off into the sea. The similarity to a carrier was further heightened by the presence of a small stone building erected at the side of the runway half-way along its length, which provided the equivalent of the navigation bridge of its Naval counterpart.

To add to my pleasure of getting back to operational flying, Frank Tyson had become Station Commander at Krendi. This made all the difference when we got down to the serious problems of the day—offensive operations.

The Luftwaffe units based in Sicily had now become decidedly shy of venturing near Malta and indeed seemed to have developed cold feet in as much as they did not even bother to try to patrol their own air space. On many occasions we flew over Sicily searching for someone with whom to pick a quarrel. We hoped, too, that the presence of our fighters, so close to their home ground, would be sufficient to lure their aircraft into the air, but even this had no effect. After several fruitless missions we decided that it was a waste of effort to go on just cruising over the Sicilian countryside and doing little else except have a look at it.

We started to experiment with the carriage of two 500 lb. bombs slung under the wings of our Spitfires similar to the manner in which Hurricanes had been fitted out for service in the Western Desert. After several trials we found that the load seemed no problem for a Spitfire to carry and the little fighter behaved as if she had been designed specifically for use as a bomber.

Anxious to put our experiments into practice we chose a small chemical factory at Pochino, in southern Sicily, as the target for our first raid with the new equipment. We took off with twelve Spitfires carrying bombs, escorted by twelve others, one of which I piloted, and set course northwards, keeping close to sea level so as not to alert the enemy radar and defences.

When we reached a position about ten miles south of the Sicilian coastline all power was used to enable us to make a rapid climb to a height of six thousand feet. At this level we flew on towards our target. Whether or not the enemy had spotted us they did not send up any fighters to intercept. It was not long before we were able to pick out landmarks on the coast and when the factory itself was sighted the twelve escorting fighters swept off to one side while the bomb-carrying Spitfires wheeled over one by one and dived vertically on to the target. In each Spitfire, with his 500 lb. lethal weapon under each wing, the pilot kept his screaming dive under control while he zeroed the bombs on target by using the normal gunsight.

One after the other the bombs rained down on the target area, dropping at regular intervals and exploding with frightening velocity. At least three made direct hits on the factory, sending tons of masonry hurtling through the air to join the twisted metal of the gutted machinery. As the last bomber began its dive I swooped down to ground level with my eleven escorting companions and raced in on the scene of destruction, raking the smoke and flames with cannon and machine-gun fire.

The vibration set up by the firing of the guns was like the tingling of newly awakened nerves. The last time I had felt such a sensation had been in combat with a ME 109 more than two years previously in the closing stages of the Battle of Britain. Although my target was now stationary and on the ground and little or no defence was being put up by the few anti-aircraft guns in the vicinity, I felt the old familiar feeling begin to take hold of me once again; that feeling which got into the blood of most men whose job it was to handle the swift-flying fighters and no matter how long aircraft and man were parted was sure to return when man and machine were once more linked together in combat.

It was not a feeling of power or a blood lust which dictated that you must destroy those who stood in your path. It was a strange, overwhelming feeling of excitement that made your mouth dry with the taste of it; your heart beat faster and your body tensed itself in its firm and unrelaxed grip.

Your hands gripped the controls as you put your fighter through its paces and the quick responses to your demands seemed to mould you more firmly into the very heart of the machine until you were not merely there with it, but firmly, and most certainly, a living, straining part of it. When fighter and pilot were as one like this you felt invincible.

But it was a feeling which only took possession for a few

fleeting moments when the thrill of the chase, the dog fight or the attack was at its height. Once it had ebbed away your brain told you once again that you were but a man—a mere microcosm of humanity—and that the fighter you flew was but a machine of nuts and bolts, of metal, subject to all man's frailties. Back to reality you felt vulnerable; even lonely. But the memory of the feeling would linger on until the next time and the time after that—if you were lucky. This is what breathed in your veins to spur you on again and again so that once more you could capture that moment of total release.

As I came alive once more at the controls of the Spitfire I swept towards the wreckage of the factory and saw the large double doors gaping invitingly from a portion of the building still left standing. Quickly, I lined up with the black cavern and fired rapid bursts through the opening. As I pulled back on the stick to lift the Spitfire above the smoke, there were clear indications that my fire power had struck home. There were signs of a large explosion and judging by the clouds of steam, followed by dense black smoke which billowed from the tall chimney and burst outwards from several of the factory windows, I was certain that I had hit a massive boiler.

Out of the corner of my eye I saw a small donkey, hitched to a tiny cart, take to its heels and make off at a furious pace down the road to Pochino, leaving nothing behind it but swirling clouds of dust. The unfortunate animal must have been struck on the behind by a stray bullet as it stood quietly beside the building because as long as I had it in view the donkey never looked back as it dashed to safety.

Re-forming, the 'bomber' aircraft, now shed of their loads, acted as escort to the twelve 'straffers' whose ammunition was spent. We set course for Malta and were back on the ground, ready to refuel, without any retaliation from the Sicilian-based enemy aircraft.

Back in the island I discovered that owing to the speed which the bomb-carrying Spitfires had accumulated in their vertical dive on the factory, a number of seats had collapsed through the immense pull of the force of gravity, exerted when they were pulled violently out of the dive. The pilots had been forced to crouch or adopt semi-standing positions in their cockpits throughout the entire flight back to base.

Following our success at Pochino we carried out a considerable number of this type of sortie during the following weeks, choosing isolated targets which were of military importance and occasionally airfields or flying-boat bases. Whether the tactical value derived from these raids was great, it is difficult to say, but it was most certainly of great morale value to the squadrons and indeed to the entire Maltese population, to feel that the R.A.F. were once again on the offensive.

The news of the Allied landings in Algeria and the great advances made by the Eighth Army along the coasts of Cyrenaica and Tripolitania was received with considerable rejoicing in Malta. No longer did we feel like the Forgotten People, isolated by thousands of miles from all hope of succour and sustenance. Instead we came back into the picture in the front line of the offensive battle opening up before the eyes of the world.

Due to Rommel's having run into trouble the Luftwaffe squadrons of transport and bomber aircraft were urgently commandeered to support the misfortunes of the Afrika Corps by carrying much needed stores and equipment from Italy and Sicily. Consequently, Malta was left comparatively free from attack. By now the Germans had learned to respect the efficiency of our radar equipment and routed their JU 52 transports from Sicily and Tunis at sea level, well clear of the island and outside the effective range of our detection gear.

When we discovered this we temporarily discarded the bomb racks and fitted on overload tanks to the Spitfires to enable long-range sweeps to be undertaken so that the German transports could be intercepted. Several sorties were reasonably successful and resulted in a number of these large, slow, tri-motored aircraft being shot down, but the German pilots had grown extremely cautious and used all their skill to outwit us.

At times our patrols took us as far afield as the battlefields of Tunisia. These long trips were never popular as they entailed flying anything up to five and a half hours in a single seater aircraft, which is not one of the most comfortable occupations to indulge in. There was also a more serious side to our dislike of the long-range sorties; normally they entailed flying at sea level, as close to the waves as it was safe to descend, for several hours. An engine failure in a Spitfire at that height meant one thing only—complete disaster.

A Spitfire was not an aircraft one could pancake on to the sea and then merely step out of the cockpit. When it hit the water it went straight to the bottom as quickly as the blade of a knife. Several pilots were lost in this way and when one realized the fate that awaited should anything go wrong, it is little wonder that there was considerable apprehension among the squadrons when the time came round for yet another sortie into Tunisia.

Now that I was completely involved in operational flying again, I began to notice a marked physiological change in myself. To begin with I felt old for the first time in my life. I had not realized until then that the cycle of pilots in the R.A.F. had changed so rapidly because nearly all the young fellows with whom I was flying had either been at school or were just learning to fly during the time of the Battle of Britain. I'm sure many of them looked on me as something of a museum piece who could be classed chronologically with Bleriot, Maurice Farman and others. A staggering thought as far as I was concerned, considering I was only twenty-six.

More worrying than that, however, was that I found I was much more concerned about my flying than I had ever been during 1940. In those epic days one would swing into battle with carefree abandon and having survived each incident, would remark without a thought: 'Gosh, we must be lucky.'

The thought of the likelihood of anything ever happening to me had very rarely ever crossed my mind. But now I found that I was planning what I would do in the event of this or that going wrong, long before the exigency could possibly arise. This started to worry me and I found that the more I tried not to think about it, the more pronounced did the thought loom up in my mind. It wasn't fear—I had already analysed that satisfactorily—it was more due to the fact that, having matured, my imagination was now much keener than it had been about two years previously. I put this down to the added experience I had gained and which I had been able to ponder over at times, perhaps, subconsciously, during the intervening period when I had handled ground duties. Eventually, I succeeded in coming to terms with this marked change in my outlook, but it was a trying experience which I could very well have done without.

The island of Lampedusa was used as a training ground for dropping bombs from Spitfires, as this target gave new members to the squadrons experience in navigating over the sea as well as of dropping bombs while coming under fire from the ground. Enemy fighters were not normally based there and flak was the only deterrent used against raiders.

On most occasions we chose the military headquarters as our target and in order to achieve the maximum amount of effect from our bombs they were fitted with a rod attachment which protruded about two feet in front of the percussion caps. The object of this device was to explode the bomb about twelve inches above the ground, when the tip of the rod struck home. As a result, a much more spectacular blast effect took place.

The operation of this method worked smoothly until the day 'Nipple' Heppell was carrying out a raid on Lampedusa when one of his bombs 'hung up' and would not free itself from under the wing. The forward attachment released itself after a time, but the back fastening remained firmly in place. This left the bomb hanging nose downwards with its two feet of rod protruding below the level of the undercarriage when it was lowered. Heppell tried desperately to shake off the bomb, banking and turning, diving and climbing, even rocking the aircraft from side to side, as he put the Spitfire through a series of complicated manœuvres. But still the bomb stuck fast. It was a hopeless situation because the Spitfire would have been blown to pieces with her undercarriage only inches off the ground had a landing been attempted.

After further repeated attempts to jettison the bomb, Heppell was ordered to climb, fly out over the sea and bale out. An air-sea rescue launch was despatched to the rendezvous point and when both aircraft and launch were in position, Heppell was radioed and informed that all was ready for his descent.

Swiftly he undid his safety harness, slid back the cockpit canopy and threw himself over the side. The pilot started to fall, gathering speed as he went. When the time came to release his chute he looked upwards as he started to float beneath the billowing canopy. A chilly spasm of fear ran along his spine. The empty Spitfire, reluctant to part company with her pilot, had started to spiral around him as he descended.

Equally horrified was the crew of the launch trying to judge the approximate position where the pilot would land in the water. No matter which direction they took, how far they went or how they turned, the rapidly falling Spitfire, with bomb plainly visible as it swung back and forth under the starboard wing, always seemed to be pointing straight at their craft. Nearer and nearer came man and machine and when collision seemed certain the launch made a frantic dash for safety as the shadow of the Spitfire passed over it and crashed into the sea. There was a tremendous explosion which sent jets of water high in the air, drenching the men in the vicinity and causing a heavy wash which violently rocked the launch as the crew brought it round for Heppell's rescue.

Within seconds Heppell dropped into the sea and almost before he had freed himself from the drag of his sodden parachute the launch was at his side, the men ready to haul him to safety.

When the weather was too bad to risk flying large formations of fighters we took off in pairs on what were known as Rhubarb Patrols. The idea behind these operations was for small forces of aircraft to freelance over enemy territory seeking out likely-looking targets on which to inflict the maximum amount of damage. Trains, railway sidings, army barracks, oil storage tanks, troop concentrations—all received visits from us. To make the patrols doubly exhilarating, both prior to and during an attack, we always flew as close to the ground as possible. This meant that one had to be wide awake and on the alert for every eventuality as the Spitfire raced on hugging the contours of the terrain.

One morning I teamed up with Tommy Smart, the commanding officer of 229 Squadron, and took off from Malta when low cloud hung over the area and rain fell in gentle showers, cutting our visibility considerably. We streaked towards the coast of Sicily and when the high cliffs hove into view started to climb until we cleared their tops. As we set course inland green countryside started to unfold beneath and with the mountains behind us we descended until it seemed as though we were skimming over the ground. Small groups of villagers gaped up open-mouthed as we roared over their homesteads or stopped in their tracks as they tended their crops in the fields.

About ten miles inland we spotted the white smoke of a train as it puffed its way laboriously through a long railway cutting. At the end of the cutting the track led into a tunnel and with a fair distance still between us and our now intended target it looked as if we would have to hurry if we were going to get within firing range in time.

Tommy and I opened our throttles and sped towards our quarry. Almost as we started to fire the last truck disappeared into the inky blackness of the tunnel mouth. We flew on and banked over the other end of the tunnel, then started to circle, waiting for the moment when the engine would steam out into daylight again. Round and round we went in tight turns, but in the long run it became obvious that the engine driver was no fool. He must have had eyes like a hawk to spot us coming up on his train from far behind and very wisely had decided to stay put in the smelly interior of the shelter rather than run the gauntlet of two irresponsible fighter pilots itching to loose off their cannon and machine-gun fire at both him and his charge. Eventually we decided to call it a day and levelling out we sped off in search of more trouble.

Several miles ahead we came on a road and wing to wing we roared along above the surface. As we approached a corner a

E

Wermacht staff car appeared, travelling at a high speed towards us. There was just time to loose off a few shots as I saw the car go completely out of control and plunge headlong into a deep ditch, the rear end pointing towards the sky, the offside wheels spinning madly as the vehicle lay half on its side and nose.

For the rest of the morning we hunted the terrain but there was little else worthy of our attention. Pointing the Spitfires' noses towards base we headed back out over the coast.

As we swooped down, prior to levelling out over the sea, I saw a small ship nosing down the coastline making for Licata harbour. Tommy saw it too and as one we banked round and down and went straight for it. No one bothered to put up any resistance. Just as we reached firing range the members of the crew on deck were joined by their companions from below and like a scrambling, milling army of ants they raced for the sides and either plunged headlong or fell in untidy heaps into the sea. Firing off several bursts at the superstructure just to show that we did mean business after all we turned again and headed for Malta.

Early in 1943 an outbreak of infantile paralysis swept the island. At one period almost a tenth of the population were suffering from some effects of it. Service personnel did not escape the scourge and one by one they disappeared into hospital to be treated. All places of public amusement were closed, meetings of more than two or three people were prohibited and the blackout went by the board as windows and doors were kept open wide in an attempt to arrest the infection.

One morning in the middle of February I woke up feeling wretched, with eyes streaming, a pain down my back, stiffness in my arms and a high temperature. Fully convinced that I had succumbed I wasted no time and drove to the large military hospital at Imtarfa. I was given what I can only describe as an exhaustive checkover, then put to bed in one of the comfortable rooms in this modern hospital, which had miraculously escaped serious damage during the blitzes, despite its commanding position on the hill overlooking Takali airfield.

About an hour later the medical officer came into the room and announced: 'No, it's not paralysis.'

I breathed a sigh of relief.

The M.O. had more to say: 'Tell me, have you been drinking any milk lately?'

One of the orders which I had observed most stringently since coming to Malta had been the one about not drinking any milk for fear of infection.

'No—most certainly not,' I replied. 'I haven't touched a drop here at all.'

The doctor wasn't satisfied.

'Think back and tell me when you last drank milk,' he requested.

Thinking hard I suddenly remembered the vast quantities of cream I had taken with porridge in Beirut and the cheese made from goat's milk of which I had been so fond.

I told him. He nodded in return—a curious mixture of sympathy and confirmation.

I was informed that this had undoubtedly been the source of the undulent fever which I had contracted. I would have to take a medical board on March 13. Until then I must rest in hospital.

The fateful day arrived but they need not have bothered. The board was only a pure formality. The only known successful remedy for undulent fever is to get out of the Mediterranean as quickly as possible. It came as no surprise when I was told I would be posted back to the U.K.

That night, after a hectic last-minute party I flew out for Gibraltar on the first stage of my journey. As the aircraft climbed away into the darkness I could see several lights twinkling below me. Because of the blackout regulations the island should have been plunged into gloom. But the sight of those lights as they flickered and finally faded from view as the aircraft plunged through the cloud base, seemed to typify the marvellous spirit of the Maltese people.

They had thrown out a challenge of defiance when at first they had stood alone. Now they were no longer so isolated, but they would go on being defiant until at last they were free again.

Their determined spirit would see to that. As I thought of the friends I had made and the good times and bad I had had I dozed off into a deep sleep. When I awoke the majestic Rock of Gibraltar stood outlined far below our starboard wing. The first flurry of turbulent air which normally swirls and eddies around the pinnacle caught hold of the fuselage and made it tremble. Slowly, the aircraft prepared to land.

11   *Prelude to D-Day*

For the purposes of air defence, Great Britain and Northern Ireland were divided into a number of operational groups. In 1943 there were six such divisions—No. 9 Group covering the north-western half of England and Wales; No. 10 Group, the south-western part; No. 11 Group, the south-eastern and London areas; No. 12 Group, the Midland and north-eastern areas; No. 13 Group, the North of England and Southern Scotland; No. 14 Group, Northern Scotland and the Orkney and Shetland Islands. There was a separate group for Northern Ireland.

The Groups were further sub-divided into what were known as Fighter Sectors, each sector being operationally responsible for all flying taking place within its area. A Fighter Operations room was to be found at each Group and Sector Headquarters, the former having no direct contact with the aircraft themselves, having been established primarily to enable the Air Officer Commanding to make the necessary dispositions and to more readily assess the reinforcing action within its command.

The sector to which I was posted as commander in November, 1943, was one of the four in No. 10 Group and covered an area extending over the whole of South Wales and the north of Devon, as well as out to sea as far as the south coast of Eire. The headquarters were situated at Fairwood Common, an airfield built on high ground about five miles west of Swansea. This, too, was to come under my direct command.

Based on Fairwood Common was a night fighter squadron equipped with Beaufighters. There was also an armament practice station to which day fighter squadrons came for three weeks at a time to polish up their air firing technique.

A detachment of an army co-operation squadron, used for exercising with Army units based near by, made up the remainder of our regularly based flying units. Besides the Fighter operations room with its attendant directional finding outstations I had control of two permanent Ground Control Interception stations, at Ripperston in Pembrokeshire and Wrafton in Devon. Overall one thousand seven hundred men and five hundred W.A.A.F. personnel came under my command.

It took some time to find my way around the station as it had been built on the dispersed principle, which meant that it was many miles from one side of the area to the other. Bit by bit I managed to unravel the whereabouts of each section in turn and, having learned what particular units were occupying which living sites, was soon able to discuss things more intelligently with my Squadron Leader Admin. and Station Adjutant.

Not long after I settled in at Fairwood, the Flying Control Officer rang me up from the control tower to say that he was in radio contact with an American B.24 bomber which was lost and running short of fuel. It had left North Africa on the previous evening bound for Portreath, in Cornwall, but on arriving over that airfield the pilot had found fog blanketing the entire area and he was forced to fly around looking for an alternative aerodrome on which to land. This had not proved easy for him because nearly all bases were shrouded in mist and many, like Portreath, were completely fogbound. Our own weather conditions were far from good when we first picked up the pilot's distress signals and although visibility was reduced to a little over one thousand yards and the cloud base stood at only two hundred feet we decided to try to bring him in.

Broadcasting a directional bearing to lead the B.24 over our airfield we waited patiently to pick up the noise of its approach. Sure enough about fifteen minutes later somewhere far above the clouds I heard the uneven throbbing of the four engines. Judging by the unhealthy sound they were making it was obvious that the aircraft's fuel supply was almost exhausted and that time was running out if we were to ensure that it landed safely.

Our next instruction was for the pilot to fly out over the sea, reducing height until he was able to see the surface of the waves. He did this and after what seemed to be an age reported that he was turning back towards Fairwood Common. In the intervening minutes the weather had worsened slightly and now clouds were rolling across the airfield, damp and threatening and because of their size and density a nightmare for any pilot attempting to bring even a fully serviceable aircraft down through them for a landing.

I caught my first glimpse of the B.24 as it skirted past the south boundary of the field; for a moment it was clearly visible as it broke out of one cloud, then it was gone from view as it plunged deep into the heart of the next grey blanket. It had been time enough, all the same, for me to see that already one of the engines had been starved of fuel; the momentary glimpse of a stationary feathered propeller was a grim reminder that the other three could soon go the same way.

Swiftly I gave the order for Very lights and rockets to be fired and within seconds they were exploding all over the place. The reflection of their brilliant light among the mist and drizzle gave a ghostly appearance to the airfield as dark shadowy shapes were thrown into savage relief among the swirling dampness. But the sudden burst of light was no help to the pilot; the cloud base was too low.

All the time we were endeavouring to lead the aircraft round the circuit so as to position it favourably for a landing on our longest runway. Lowering the undercarriage and flaps the pilot just about made the grade on one occasion when, as he had almost given up hope, he caught a fleeting glimpse of the runway. He was just a fraction too late and what happened in the ensuing seconds seemed almost unbelievable to those of us standing on top of the control tower.

Four bodies were seen to leave the B.24 through the open bomb well doors and hurtle unchecked towards the ground from a height of only a few hundred feet. One after the other they disappeared behind a large hangar. With sinking hearts we realized there had been no sign of any of the parachutes even beginning to open. Automatically dismissing the four foolhardy members of the crew as having plunged to their deaths and assuming the aircraft to have been completely abandoned I waited to see where it was going to crash.

The B.24 careered over the administrative buildings, missing them by several feet and headed straight for the guard house which stood beside the south gate. The horror of what was likely to happen when it finally struck the building almost made me shut my eyes to avoid seeing the impact. In my mind's eye I could see the explosion, followed by the pall of dark smoke, the flames and the relentless crackling of the burning wreckage.

Then I saw a wing start to raise itself feebly in an effort to bank the aircraft away from the building. Almost together several of those standing beside me shouted in amazement: 'Good God, the pilot must still be in there!'

There was insufficient time and, no doubt, not enough power left in the B.24 to carry it clear of the guard house. As cleanly as a knife it ploughed through the small building and carried on for around fifty yards before finally burying its nose in a high, grassy bank. The main part of the fuselage and the tail, still trembling from the force of the impact, pointed towards the sky.

Bob Sankey, the station engineer officer, had already dashed off on his motor cycle to where the four bodies had been seen to fall and I raced to my car to make my way to the crashed aircraft. Surprisingly, I found the pilot in fairly good shape, having had the sense to keep his safety harness firmly fastened. Undoubtedly this had saved him from death, or severe injury, because the remaining crew member, the flight engineer, had been thrown out through the windscreen when the aircraft had come to a halt. There was little anyone could do for him and he died later from his injuries.

When Bob reached the spot where he expected to find the four corpses, he found instead that he was staring at three discarded parachutes and an American civilian, appropriately attired in horn-rimmed glasses and clutching a large box under one arm.

To our amusement we discovered later that this contained cigars.

Expecting that the airborne arrival might be suffering from shock after his unorthodox plunge to earth Bob approached cautiously. He was greeted with a genial smile.

'Hi, fella. Good to see you. Is this England I'm standing on?' enquired the round bespectacled face.

'No, it's Wales, I'm afraid,' replied Bob, rather taken aback.

'Oh.' The American seemed crestfallen. 'I guess that's just too bad.' He shook his head sadly, like someone who has followed a carefully laid-out set of directions, then discovered he's taken a wrong turning.

'Yes, that's just too bad,' he repeated. 'I've never been to England before and I was kinda lookin' forward to visitin' there.'

'Well, we're not all that far away!' Bob proceeded to inform him, when he suddenly realized how ridiculous the conversation was becoming. After all he had come expecting to find bodies, not to talk of geography.

'Look, where are the others?' asked Bob, gesturing impatiently at the empty parachutes.

'Oh, don't you go troublin' yourself about them. They're all right. Look, they're over there beside the coffee waggon.' He pointed through the mist in the direction of the main road which ran through the centre of the station.

Followed by the carefree American civilian Bob set off at a brisk trot. He found them standing around the mobile Y.M.C.A. tea waggon, drinking steaming mugs of brew and exchanging jokes with the girls behind the counter. They seemed little the worse for wear following their close shave with death and as they drained the last of their tea told Bob how all their parachutes had opened just in time to take the initial strain before they landed on the soft heath.

The Y.M.C.A. waggon had been travelling along the road when first one, then two, then three and finally, to the delight and amazement of the tea girls, a fourth individual had dropped down through the mist and thudded in a circle round them. True to form the girls' first thoughts were for their unorthodox customers and within sixty seconds of their arrival, mugs of tea were being pressed into their hands.

One of the Americans was particularly impressed by the speed of the service. He kept shaking his head in astonishment and telling Bob: 'You guys sure have things buttoned up well over here. Do you always have tea ready like this when someone's coming in by 'chute? Real crazy, that's what I call it, man . . . real crazy.'

At this point his companions would murmur agreement and nod enthusiastically. It was almost possible to see the look of relief on Bob's face when several of us drove up to join him and share the responsibilities of dealing with the happy-go-lucky Americans.

One of my first acts after arriving at Fairwood was to call on the Lord Mayor of Swansea, Alderman W. Harries, to pay my respects. I found that, like myself, he had just taken over from his predecessor which, in itself, seemed to forge a link in the bond of friendship which we immediately struck up.

He was a delightful person, always willing to help and entertain us whenever he found it possible. It came as a great shock to many service personnel in the area when he was killed in a motor accident before he had completed his term of office.

However, on my first visit to the Mansion House, the Lord Mayor informed me that, although he had always taken the keenest interest in the Royal Air Force, he had never visited an aerodrome. Would it be possible for me to arrange this? he queried. Naturally, I invited him to call at Fairwood Common any time he wished.

Next day the telephone rang in my office. It was the Lord Mayor. 'Look, would it be all right if I came on Sunday and I would like very much to bring my wife and daughter with me for, you see, I'm only in office for one year and I want them to get full advantage of all my privileges.'

Such was his charm that he made the request in one long breath as if he had spent hours plucking up sufficient courage to ring and then when he did, had decided to get it over with as quickly as possible. I agreed without hesitation.

On the following Sunday he arrived, complete with chain of office, his charming wife and attractive daughter. There was also a small retinue of retainers and we set to with a will to entertain everyone. Everything went off extremely well except when Colonel Helme, a delightful old gentleman who lived near by and who had been an honorary member of the officers' mess for many years, succeeded in tipping over an entire row of seats, all occupied, during the church service. There was considerable confusion when this happened, with a jumble of bodies on the floor, entangled in each other's arms and legs. Being inside a church didn't help and there was silent amusement on many faces as everyone sorted themselves out and tried to regain their seats, attempting all the time to look as if nothing untoward had happened. The poor colonel was most embarrassed, but later in the day when it was time for lunch in the mess a few stiff drinks helped to put his mind at rest.

Another person whom we were honoured to have as an honorary member of the mess was Sir Arthur Whitten-Brown, best remembered for the epic flight in which he partnered Sir John Alcock in 1919 and succeeded in flying across the Atlantic for the first time. It took them sixteen hours twelve minutes to get from Newfoundland to Ireland in a converted Vickers Vimy bomber, powered by two Rolls-Royce Eagle engines.

Teddy told me the story of how he came to make the flight. During the First World War, as Lieutenant Whitten-Brown he had the misfortune to be captured by the Germans. During his enforced stay in a prisoner of war camp he spent his time developing a system of astral navigation—a forerunner of the astro navigation practised today.

On the termination of hostilities he was posted to Air Ministry, in the Supply Branch. Although he had plenty of work to do in this job he also found time to write articles for one of the leading aeronautical periodicals on the subject of his study in astro-navigation.

The normal course of his duties took him frequently to aircraft factories and it was during one such visit to Vickers at Weybridge that he was shown the special Vimy aircraft which was being prepared as an entrant for the *Daily Mail* prize of ten thousand pounds offered for the first heavier-than-air machine to fly across the Atlantic.

'Whom do you intend to use as navigator?' enquired Teddy.

'Oh, we haven't chosen anyone yet,' replied the Vickers' official.

Teddy thought for a few seconds, then said: 'By the way, have you read any of my articles on astro-navigation in *Flight*?'

The official was completely taken aback. 'Good Heavens, Brown—did you write those? I hadn't realized that. Come over here one minute. . . .'

In this way Teddy's selection as navigator was settled on the spot although it was kept a dark secret for some time afterwards. He applied for special leave, which was granted without hesitation, and sailed for America with Jack Alcock.

The flight was not without its moments of excitement. The windmill driving the wireless power dynamo broke off when they had been airborne for only a little over an hour; icing in one of the carburettors almost spelt disaster on another occasion when they were only half-way across. But, undaunted, the two aviators pressed on regardless and, as the world knows, landed in a bog in Galway.

Teddy showed me the message pad used during the flight and it was fascinating to see the record of messages passed from navigator to pilot during the flight as vocal-intercommunication was not used.

'0800. Port engine started up,' records the first message.

'Steer 072 degrees M,' reads another.

'Have a sandwich?' yet another.

'I think you are too far north, plus ten degrees.' So it goes on, page by page, each tersely written message showing the written thoughts and conveying the feelings of these two heroes as they were actually in the process of making aerial history.

Even the quality of the handwriting shows perfectly the particular feelings at any given time. One entry reads, 'That was a narrow squeak' and this is barely decipherable because of the shaky handwriting. I asked Teddy about this and was told that it had been scribbled down just after they had spun down from around eight thousand feet, owing to ice having formed on the wings and when Alcock had only just succeeded in righting the aircraft before it finally hit the sea.

Towards the end of the notes is a delightful tell-tale remark. 'I'm not sure just where this is—fly down the next railway line you see until we find a station.'

Alcock and Brown were not the only people who were reduced on occasions to having to read the name off a railway station signboard in order to determine their position. When these indicating boards were removed during the war it caused quite a few additional problems to some pilots. I was once reduced to coming down low enough to read the name off the front of a bus which was heading for a large town, in order to satisfy myself about my own position during one difficult flight.

We celebrated the twenty-fifth anniversary of the historic flight at Fairwood and felt greatly privileged that Teddy was with us as guest of honour. Sir John Alcock was, unfortunately, killed in a flying accident in the year following the flight.

One of the biggest headaches at Fairwood was dealing with the cattle and wild ponies that grazed on the common. Being common ground we could not force the farmers to keep their beasts away from the premises and wire fences seemed totally inadequate to deter the animals from wandering on and off the landing ground as and when they pleased. We tried encircling the landing area with a wire through which a small charge of electricity was passed, but the sheep and cattle simply loved this new device and spent long periods brushing against it, thoroughly enjoying the tingling sensation.

The ponies were completely wild and came principally from Caeffyn Bryn, a hill quite close to Fairwood. On cold nights they flocked on to the aerodrome in droves to squat on the runways where they found it relatively warmer and more comfortable than the surrounding hills and valleys. None of them was ever hit by an aircraft making a landing in darkness, although there were many near misses and accidents, only averted by sharp-eyed pilots who managed to take evasive action at the last possible moments.

The distance between the accommodation sites and the various places of duty was a constant source of annoyance and discomfort to many of the personnel on the station. Owing to a lack of cars and lorries everyone had to walk or cycle, if they were fortunate enough to get hold of a bicycle, between their place of work and sleeping quarters. In many cases these were several miles apart. As the airmen and airwomen were only issued with two pairs of footwear, one of these was always at the cobbler's shop being re-soled and heeled. On many occasions the second pair had completely worn out before the first pair had been repaired and were again ready for use.

The W.A.A.F. were hardest hit of all as their living sites were furthest from the headquarters block. Presumably the architect who originally planned the lay-out had been endowed with puritanical morals and decided to banish the girls to a purdah-like existence as far as he possibly could. Unfortunately the only two sites which suffered any damage during the war were Nos. 4 and 5—the two occupied by the W.A.A.F.

During one air raid which took place nearly a year before my arrival the only bomb which dropped anywhere near the airfield made a direct hit on No. 4 site, killing and injuring several of the girls as they slept. But in April, 1944, disaster struck again.

Darkness had fallen when I was told that a Halifax four-engined bomber was in trouble near by. Two of its engines had packed in and flying control had prepared a full emergency to help the pilot get his aircraft down on the ground. Shortly after I arrived at the control tower the Halifax started to lose height quickly as it flew around the circuit. There was little the pilot could do and with a dull thump the bomber crashed straight into the middle of No. 5 site. There was no explosion, just the tearing and crumbling of the masonry as the aircraft plunged headlong through everything in its path before coming to rest on its belly. Then an ominous silence.

I got over to where the mutilated aircraft lay and met the crew coming towards me. They were quite surprised and also completely unaware that they had hit anything. But, clambering back into the site itself through a gap in the hedge made by the crashing aircraft, a scene of utter desolation met our gaze.

Three low stone sleeping blocks full of W.A.A.F. personnel had been completely razed to the ground, while two others were severely damaged and seemed in danger of imminent collapse. The sound of moaning and groaning came to us from beneath the piles of debris where many of the girls were trapped. The sounds of those in pain and fear seemed all the more terrible because of the darkness, broken only by a number of small fires starting up where coal stoves, which had been burning in all the destroyed huts, had been tipped over and smashed against the woodwork.

Teams of medical orderlies were quickly on the scene, accompanied by rescue squads and soon everyone was busy heaving aside large sections of plaster and bricks in an effort to reach the victims. The Group Nursing Sister, Sister Stone, who had been visiting the station earlier in the day and was staying overnight, took charge of the first-aid side and seemed to be everywhere at once, tending injuries or administering morphia to those in distress. Despite the holocaust around them, made all the more terrifying by the darkness and the flickering of the fires, coupled with the frantic dancing lights of the hand torches, there was no sign of panic breaking out. Everyone, including the W.A.A.F. officers and N.C.O.'s, displayed a remarkable degree of calm and calculated efficiency.

Rescue operations dragged on throughout the night, with the seriously injured being taken in whatever transport could be commandeered to one of the larger emergency hospitals in Swansea after receiving first-aid treatment in our own, but by now overcrowded, sick quarters. Many of the girls were in deep shock when pulled from the debris. It must have been a frightening experience for them; one minute they had been fast asleep in their barrack rooms; the next they were awakening in utter chaos, in the dust and rubble, many of them pinned in their beds by broken beams or large chunks of masonry.

When dawn broke over the station and the weak light showed for the first time the complete scene of destruction I was only amazed that more people had not been killed outright. Shortly after daybreak the last of the girls was freed and the grim total of casualties was handed to me. One W.A.A.F. had been killed, eighteen were seriously injured and nearly forty were suffering from shock and other injuries.

Anyone who had tended to take the presence of the W.A.A.F.'s for granted before the crash soon changed his ideas when the station got down to work again later in the day. The domestic services were the most seriously affected as many of the girls were employed in the various messes or cookhouses. For several days officers and airmen alike had their meals in the vast airmen's dining hall, an arrangement which worked admirably and which also presented a first-class opportunity for all ranks to get to know each other better.

Towards the end of April enemy activity increased in the area and squadrons operating from Fairwood had their fair share of aerial combat—much of it highly successful. We presumed that the majority of the raiders were employed mainly in a reconnaissance role because preparations for a full-scale attempt to regain a foothold on the Continent were by now well advanced. It was only to be expected that the Germans would be anxious to find out how things were going over in Britain. We ourselves were kept well in the dark as to what actually was being planned, but it was obvious that immense preparations were being made. Landing craft, merchant shipping, stores, troops and ammunition were all being concentrated around our coasts.

I was not to wonder and speculate for long. In the middle of May I was promoted to the rank of Acting Group Captain and sent to Bentley Priory, at Stanmore in Middlesex, as 'Operations 1' of the Allied Expeditionary Air Force Headquarters under the command of Air Chief Marshal Sir Trafford Leigh-Mallory.

The Priory had been the home of Fighter Command for many years and had been chosen as the most suitable spot on which to superimpose the control of the Allied Expeditionary Air Force, owing to the mass of communications which emanated from it.

My job, roughly speaking, was to supervise the overall control of all R.A.F. fighter squadrons detailed to take part in the great offensive against the Continent. A colonel of the United States Army Air Corps sat alongside me and looked after his country's fighter forces.

Immediately I arrived I became 'bigoted'. This term was applied to all those who were in the know as to the plans for the impending invasion and it was a state to which only a few were admitted. After being 'bigoted' one was not allowed to expose oneself to any threat of capture and consequently there was never any question of being allowed to fly over enemy territory for fear of being shot down. My period of 'bigotry' was to be short-lived, however, for D-Day took place less than three weeks after my arrival at Stanmore.

The nerve centre of this vast aerial war machine was situated in the A.E.A.F. war room, a small and thoroughly cramped room leading off from the main underground Fighter Command operations centre. Around three walls were various maps showing dispositions of forces, intended lanes of approach to the Normandy Coast, points of departure of the various elements making up the attacking force and intended points of advances to be made after the Expeditionary Force landed. The fourth wall was a complete battery of telephones all placed behind a soundproof glass screen.

As the original D-Day, June 5, drew near the faces of the Service chiefs grew more tense and strained as they studied the mass of meteorological material which was being put before them. Fair weather was one of the essentials if the effort was to be a success. Many of the convoys had to come from distant ports, some as far away as the north-west coast of England.

By June 4 many of these had already got under way and the last-minute postponement of the invasion put a tremendous onus on the escorting Naval ships as all the hundreds of landing craft and their escorts, which already had started on their momentous journey, had to be recalled visually.

It would have been disastrous to have broken radio silence. Rushing around like sheepdogs engaged in rounding up their flock the little ships of the Navy succeeded in stopping the fore-runners of the main force before they became too far committed to turn back. All that night a gale raged with alarming ferocity, turning landing craft into torture chambers for the tightly-packed troops trying to get some sleep while beneath them the waves crashed against the thin plates and made the vessels roll and plunge incessantly. During the early hours of daylight on the 5th the stormy weather showed signs of abating and General Eisenhower made his decision—the full attack would be made the next day.

Large numbers of bombers carried out raids and troop carry-ing sorties during the night, and light bombers and fighters were standing by to take off before dawn so as to be over the beach-heads in time to lend support to our attacking forces when they went ashore. All Air Force Commands had previously carried out an intensive offensive against the railways, roads and bridges leading into the bridgehead area.

This plan had to be extremely carefully worked out many months before so as not to give the Germans any cause to believe that this particular area was being dealt with in preference to any other. For that reason three times the number of bombs had to be dropped on other targets not directly connected with the D-Day landings in order to confuse the enemy's interpretation of where the expected major landing might be.

Until a late hour on the night of June 5/6 the War Room and Operations Room was the scene of considerable activity as senior officers of all three Services came and went, checking on and reporting the progress of the invasion fleet. As I had to be on duty at dawn I went to bed to snatch a few hours' sleep. When I re-entered the War Room at 4 a.m. I found it nearly deserted and next door, in the Operations Room, there was the same atmosphere of inactivity, almost of apathy. Two weary looking plotters casually pushed raid blocks across the plotting table on which was pictured a large scale map of the English Channel and its bordering coastlines. Three operations officers leaned over the wooden railing which ran round the raised balcony. They seemed almost asleep.

All this came as a great surprise to me, for I had fully expected the place to be crammed with Commanders-in-Chief and other members of the Services hierarchy. Nudging an American captain on the arm I asked: 'What's happening now?'

He slowly turned his head, yawned and scratched aimlessly behind one ear. 'Well,' he drawled, 'I guess they should just about be paddling ashore right now.'

He turned away and seemed to go to sleep again. Three hours later the B.B.C.'s 7 a.m. news broadcast confirmed his guess. History was being made on the other side of the Channel but below ground in Bentley Priory, where much of it had been planned and meticulously executed, it could have been just another ordinary day.

Later in the morning I was just about to enter the War Room when the door opened and the Commander-in-Chief emerged accompanied by someone whom I took at first to be a senior Naval officer. As I stood aside to allow them to pass I suddenly realized to whom Leigh-Mallory was speaking. It was King George VI who had just been shown the plots of the progress being made by our forces. Accompanying him were General Smuts, Winston Churchill and Anthony Eden. For a moment I thought I was dreaming and I could hardly bring myself to realize that those eminent men could possibly be standing in the corridor of our operations block within a few feet of me and with others merely passing to and fro around them quite unconcernedly going about their normal business. There had been no warning—not even a whispered rumour—that a Royal visit had been intended.

The office next door to mine was occupied by an American, Colonel Bagby, who was responsible for supervising the staff angle of the transport aircraft employed in carrying the airborne and parachute troops. Bagby was fifty-two years of age and his big grouse was that because of this he was not allowed to join a front line fighting unit.

'Instead,' he used to moan persistently, 'I'm stuck in this mouldy office pushing a bloody pen around all day.'

On the night of June 5 Bagby completed his duty and left.

Next day he did not turn up and there was still no sign of him on the 8th or 9th. Leigh-Mallory was furious and threatened all sorts of punishments when he was able to lay his hands on Bagby, for deserting his post at such a critical time. It did not matter to the Commander-in-Chief that Bagby's second-in-command was manning the post quite capably in his superior's sudden absence.

On the morning of the 10th there was still no sign of the missing colonel, but later in the day as I sat in my office there was a knock on the door and the familiar wrinkled face, creased even more so because of a broad grin, appeared round the corner.

I greeted him enthusiastically and before he had an opportunity to say anything asked him where he had been. 'The Chief's been tearing his hair out wondering what had become of you,' I added.

Bagby grinned even more widely. 'There was no real need for anyone to be worrying about me,' he said. 'I just wanted to get a little excitement out of this goddam war so I bummed a ride with those paratroop boys. I've been fighting like hell over in the Cotentin Peninsula ever since and just managed to get a ride back on one of the landing boats comin' home.'

The grin vanished and he looked strangely thoughtful. 'Is he really mad at me?' he asked.

The colonel was duly put on the carpet and given a severe dressing down by his superiors. At the same time this was no more than a formality because he was also congratulated most heartily when he told the full story of his adventure. It was an incredibly brave, but nevertheless foolhardy thing to have done; not only had Bagby not seen active service since 1918, but he had never jumped by parachute before, even in the daylight, let alone at night. He had certainly been in the thick of things because the batch of paratroopers he went with were among the first dropped on the Cherbourg Peninsula that night.

A large turreted building called Stanmore Hall, standing about a mile down the road from Bentley Priory, served as an officers' mess for the Headquarters' staff. Being a joint R.A.F.– United States Army Air Corps affair, we were extremely well fed. Our American friends supplied all their own rations which were considerably better than ours and as a result we benefited by their generosity.

In spite of the large appearance of Gremlin Castle, our name given to the Hall, there were few bedrooms in it and most of us had to be billeted with families living in and around Stanmore. I was particularly fortunate as I found myself staying in the local inn whose proprietor and wife were the very essence of kindness. I also acquired a bicycle which I used to pedal to and from the pub and my office. This contraption, for that's the only suitable word to describe it, must have been fitted with square ball bearings because one had to stand on the pedals all the time to make it go, even while travelling down a steep hill.

Bill Urmston, a Group Captain intelligence officer at Bentley Priory, was the proud possessor of a broken down little car and after seeing my struggles with the bicycle several times as he chugged past on his way to and from work, offered me a lift.

Bill owned a large cattle ranch in Mexico and had returned to Britain in 1939 as he was still a member of the Air Force Officers Reserve. An unfortunate accident had happened to him many years previously when, during a duck shooting expedition, his gun fired accidentally and blew off his left hand. However, he managed well enough with an artificial limb and was quite capable of driving a car.

On one particularly wet day when we were leaving the mess after lunch I made a sprint for the car and wrenched open the door. The force of my pull was so great that the whole thing came away in my hand. In lashing rain we both struggled to fit it on again and thankfully got inside the car. Then the self-starter refused to function and, being the passenger, I got out and pushed for a considerable distance before the little car's engine burst into life. I was now almost completely soaked through and, as we set off, not a word was spoken as we both inwardly fumed at the car's idiosyncrasies. Before long the next accident happened—the one and only windscreen wiper went flying away as we were travelling at a fairly brisk speed along the main road.

Bill braked and managed to bring his vehicle to a halt. Reversing was made more awkward because of the pelting rain blotting out his rear view and amid angry squawks from the horns of cars approaching fast behind us, we made our way, backwards, to the spot where the wiper had broken off. Again I got out, not caring now about trying to keep dry, and started a search of the roadway and the surrounding bank. Eventually, assisted by Bill, the wiper was located embedded in a clump of grass. With one of the many pieces of string Bill always seemed to have in the car this was replaced and we set off once more.

The rest of the journey was uneventful until we drew up outside the Priory. Bill switched off the engine and opened his door ready to make a quick dash through the rain. At that instant his artificial hand fell off and dropped straight into a large puddle.

One evening in June I dined with Colonel Helme who had come to London from Swansea for a few days and after our meal we went on to a friend's flat in Mount Street. About 10.30 p.m. the steady droning noise of a low flying aircraft came to us from almost directly overhead.

'That fellow's asking for trouble,' remarked our alarmed host. He turned to me: 'Do you think he's one of ours?'

I listened, straining hard to pick up a familiar engine beat. Suddenly the noise stopped and there was complete silence. A couple of seconds later an enormous explosion rent the air, violently shaking the furniture and ornaments in the flat.

We looked sadly at each other.

'Whoever it was, he's had it now, I'm afraid,' remarked Colonel Helme. I nodded sympathetic agreement. Enemy or friend, a human being had died a horrible death.

How wrong we were. The aerial intruder was pilotless. What we had heard was the first of the V.1 bombs to reach the London area. Soon they would become hated and dreaded by those who lived in constant fear of their silent attack.

To be perfectly honest, the V.1's frightened me much more than anything else throughout the entire war. There was something so horribly impersonal about them and their course was so dreadfully unpredictable. Many harrowing tales have been told about experiences during the period when first the V.1's and then the V.2's kept up their reign of terror, but one of the most remarkable encounters I came across involved one of the officers from Fighter Command headquarters.

This officer had been ill for several months and was called before the Central Medical Board in Kelvin House for an interview. On leaving there he was walking along Goodge Street towards Tottenham Court Road when a V.1 exploded on the corner of the street and blew him clean off his feet. Fortunately he was not injured and managed to continue on his way to Adastral House in Kingsway where he had to report the result of his medical examination.

He had almost reached the foot of Kingsway and was on the point of turning into the corner entrance to Adastral House when for no apparent reason he glanced upwards.

He was just in time to see another V.1 grazing the corner of Bush House and making straight for the spot on which he stood. Like everyone else in the street he flung himself face downwards on the pavement and, for a moment, it felt as though he had suddenly been thrown into a vacuum as the shock waves of the explosion spread outwards. The bomb had exploded on the corner of Adastral House within several yards of where he lay.

Once more he was miraculously unhurt, although ten people within fifty yards of him, and all around him too, had been killed outright. Deciding to abandon his visit to the Air Ministry he set off for the R.A.F. Club in Piccadilly in search of something to still his nerves. As he reached Piccadilly Circus yet another V.1 struck the top of the Regent Palace Hotel almost above him. By now he was a bag of nerves, and making for the Underground he took the first train out to Stanmore where I saw him less than an hour later trying to drink a cup of tea in the mess.

Bits of rubble, dust and small pieces of glass were sticking to his uniform, his neck and his hair, and the poor man was trembling so much that he had to give up trying to swallow the tea. The contents of the cup kept on spilling and no sooner had I filled it up for him again than his shaking hand forced the tea to slop over the edge once more. Although his nerves had taken a severe beating Lady Luck must have kept a special eye on him that day because it must have been rare indeed for someone to escape three times from V.1 explosions within such a short space of time.

Towards the end of August, 1944, the Allied Forces had recaptured a considerable portion of the north and north-west regions of France and the Supreme Commander, General Dwight Eisenhower, decided to move his main headquarters across to that area. A certain element of A.E.A.F. personnel were to accompany Supreme Headquarters—S.H.A.E.F., as it was better known—to act as a liaison link until A.E.A.F. headquarters moved over. I was delighted when I learned that I was to be one of the element.

A large expanse of parkland surrounding a massive brick school building was requisitioned at Jouloville, a small village on the coast of the Manche, lying about ten miles south of Granville. The nearest airfield was near Avranches and after landing there with some of my colleagues we made our way to Jouloville by road, past the wreckage of hundreds of vehicles left abandoned after the severe fighting. I was struck by the number of British cars and vans among the discarded German material. All had Werhmacht markings on them, and no doubt many were vehicles which had been abandoned by the unlucky British Expeditionary Force when it was forced to evacuate the Continent at Dunkirk in 1940.

Everything was in a state of considerable confusion at Jouloville but as the days wore on some semblance of order was restored although it was many weeks before the headquarters was once again in complete control of affairs. It was during this period that I first met General Eisenhower. From the first moment of our meeting in his caravan beside the headquarters site I liked him and it was not long before this feeling turned to admiration. Everyone who worked with him held the same high opinion of the General. His tact, charm of manner, and deep interest in his men's welfare endeared him to all our hearts.

There was little love lost, however, between General Eisenhower and General George Patton, who commanded one of the U.S. Army Corps, although the Supreme Commander did express admiration from time to time of the inexorable manner in which the latter prosecuted the war. Patton was extremely independent and advanced so rapidly that many of the decisions were made purely by himself and on a number of occasions it appeared as if he had conveniently forgotten to inform headquarters of his progress.

At such times General Eisenhower kept his feelings in check until the day when Patton overstepped the mark. Eisenhower had issued specific instructions to him to by-pass the Brest Peninsula and instead continue advancing to the east. No acknowledgement was received and finally, with Eisenhower close to exploding with anger, our own reconnaissance aircraft were ordered up to search for Patton and his army who were already in the process of mopping up the port of Brest itself.

Whenever Eisenhower found himself passing through a period of particular stress he would take to the air in a light aircraft and fly around for a short time, allowing the smooth joy of effortless flight to banish his cares and worries. When he climbed into his aircraft after fuming over Patton's failings he was indeed an angry man although, as he had already proved himself to be a quite capable pilot, we all knew that once he took off his rage would start to subside.

He had only been airborne for several minutes when the engine stopped abruptly. It was a clear day and several of us who had been watching him put his small aircraft through its paces now stared, with bated breath, as he went into a forced glide and dropped, swiftly, but silently towards the ground. We followed his progress until the aircraft dropped out of sight behind a row of sand dunes and when we got to the spot found it embedded nose-first in the soft sand.

Eisenhower was still in the cockpit, but it only took several seconds for us to release the hatch and help him out on to firmer ground. He had given his ankle a severe twist at the moment of impact, but there were plenty of willing hands to help him back to a car and rush him to headquarters for medical treatment. Despite the accident and his subsequent discomfort we found Eisenhower had now forgiven Patton for his most recent lapse and the dauntless General continued pressing on with his army towards Paris.

Thanks to General Eisenhower I was given the opportunity of visiting the United States, early in 1945, to attend a course of instruction at the Army and Navy Staff College. This was a fascinating time for me in which I spent periods in Florida, Kansas, Newport, Rhode Island and in the major cities of New York and Washington, D.C.

The news of V.E. Day came to me in Washington and the British members of the course prepared themselves for full celebrations. We fully expected to find crowds of people thronging the streets or cheering themselves hoarse in front of the White House or the Capitol Building. We were completely wrong. The only people, apart from ourselves, who seemed to be taking any advantage of the occasion were the pub keepers and the licensed vendors—all the bars and liquor stores throughout the city were closed.

By their complete lack of emotion the American people were showing that, as far as they were concerned, the job was only half done. Their time for celebration would come when the part of the conflict which was closer to their own hearts was cleared up—the war against Japan.

My six-month stay in the United States over, I set sail for Britain again, aboard the *Queen Mary*. Back home I was posted to a staff job at Watnall, near Nottingham, Headquarters No. 12 Group, the Fighter Group responsible for the Midlands. V.J. Day was announced six weeks later and in common with everyone else who had lived, breathed and fought war since 1939, a tremendous feeling of relief swept over me, now that hostilities had definitely come to an end.

The celebrations came fast and furious in the months that followed but, as the initial feeling of being at peace started to wear off and the future of the Service began to mould itself into a less warlike shape, there was plenty of work to be done. The cutting down in size of the Royal Air Force meant a corresponding reduction in the number of senior ranks being retained so I was not in the least bit surprised when I was informed, late in November, that I was soon to lose my acting rank of Group Captain.

'However, old chap,' I was informed, 'there's quite a good Wing Commander's job in the offing if you're interested—Air Attaché in Dublin.'

I was quick to respond. 'Good Heavens, I'd voluntarily drop a couple of ranks to get a job like that.'

The postings officer smiled. 'Now, let me see . . .' he paused, shuffling through some papers . . . 'there are certain qualifications needed for this post. We're looking for a Scotsman who is prepared to marry and settle down with a wife who should be white and preferably not Irish. Can you meet that?'

'I might just be able to make it,' I answered, nodding my head slowly.

In January, 1946, I flew into Dublin to face a new way of life.

12 *A touch of the blarney*

The joy of getting across to a place like Dublin after the war-time restrictions which both Margaret and I had been forced to put up with, in common with everyone else, was almost too good to be believed. Unfortunately a great number of our friends soon learned we were over there and this led to a steady stream of visitors pouring over to stay with us. It had a funny side, all the same.

Having lived for about the past five years without eating any really decent meals, the first thing they always wanted to do upon arrival was to celebrate by eating the largest amount of fancy food they could find available. As a result they soon developed a complaint aptly known as 'Dublin tummy' which was brought on by the richness of the juicy steaks and the quantities of double cream. This made it necessary for us to arrange to keep one day free for our visitors so they would have every chance of recovery. It was usually the day after their arrival.

My office was in the office of the United Kingdom Representative in Eire, in Mount Street, regarded at the time to be one of Dublin's more salubrious districts. It was a narrow street and when I arrived it was almost completely blocked by a line of hideous looking air-raid shelters sitting in the middle of the road. They had been erected so that there was just sufficient space for slow moving vehicles to squeeze past on each side.

For over a year the city authorities seemed to ignore them until, no doubt, due to the sheer volume of complaints there must have been concerning their nuisance value, they decided to demolish them. One morning a large crane, complete with a heavy metal ball suspended on a long chain, arrived in the street and got down to work. Like some powerful monster, bent on destroying everything standing in its path, the crane swept forward relentlessly, swinging the metal ball backwards and forwards against the walls of the shelters.

It was surprising just how easily the one-time air-raid shelters tumbled to the ground. As I watched their demolition being accomplished with such great ease I wondered just how effective they would have been in protecting those who might have been forced to use them in the event of an air raid.

The jobs I had to do as Air Attaché were many and varied. I was accredited to the country as the military Air Attaché, but I also had to handle all aspects of civilian aviation as well. As far as the Irish Air Corps was concerned it had been almost decimated as a result of the war because they had not been able to get any new aircraft. When I arrived they only had a few pre-war aircraft, plus a couple of Royal Air Force Hurricanes which had force landed in Eire during the war and had been commandeered. Although they seemed to use these aircraft constantly it was not to any great effect.

They were extremely anxious to bring their Air Force completely up to date and I made enquiries regarding what type of jobs they wished the new aircraft to undertake. Their main aim was to set up some organization to look after fishery protection while at the same time have some means of carrying out convenient aerial photography and reconnaissance. Towards this end my predecessor, Archie Boyd, had already negotiated with A. V. Roe and Company for them to buy three new Avro Anson 19's.

I knew from my own experience that these were highly practical aircraft as I had an official R.A.F. Anson based at Dublin for my own use. Sergeant Milne was the aircraft fitter who looked after this machine, tending it with all the loving care that a mother gives to her baby. He was an excellent character and in great demand by the Irish Air Corps. Had it not been for his skill there would have been many occasions when some of their aircraft would not have been able to take off and, as a result of his technical knowledge, his services were being constantly requested.

Shortly after the Ansons arrived and went into service the Air Corps decided they wanted to establish a form of air defence. It was not exactly clear why they wanted to do this or what reasons compelled them to spend a large sum of money in equipping such a force for no real purpose, but in those days it was considered a fashionable thing to do. I agreed to search for some Spitfires, but unfortunately, after an extensive hunt, failed to locate any that were readily available. However, I did manage to lay my hands on a dozen Supermarine Seafires—the Fleet Air Arm version of the Spitfire. The design was exactly the same except that the Seafire had a strengthened fuselage and a large hook beneath the tail so that it was suitable for carrier landings. Nevertheless, the Irish Air Corps was perfectly happy to accept these—with the hooks removed.

The Seafires were stored at Sydenham, a small airfield near Belfast, and I arranged to fly up there so that I would have an opportunity of piloting one of the newly acquired aircraft down to Baldonnel where the Irish Air Corps had its headquarters. It was a delight to be back at familiar controls and despite the difference in name it needed no use of my imagination to tell me I was handling a Spitfire again. Unfortunately the journey was all too short and after putting the Seafire through its paces in a variety of ways, somewhat reluctantly I prepared to touch down at Baldonnel.

However, I had the opportunity of handling the Seafire on several occasions as I demonstrated its capabilities to the Air Corps and after some preliminary instruction a couple of Irish pilots were able to go up solo. Everyone seemed happy and an order was placed for the remaining eleven.

The signing of the contract was conducted in what can only be described as typically Irish fashion. Eire is a wonderful country in which to live, but highly exasperating if you are attempting to negotiate any sort of business deal. Eventually, after considerable delays, the necessary formalities were completed. The time arrived when it became necessary to have the signature of a senior member of the Defence Forces Staff on the master document of the contract. Although I had got to know this person fairly well I found him extremely difficult to pin down when it came to arranging a meeting between us to finalize the business. Several days went past before I was lucky enough to telephone his office while he was actually there.

'Good morning, sir,' I announced cheerfully, trying to hide the sense of urgency in my voice which I felt sure might make him decide to delay matters even further. 'I've got the final details of the contract for the Seafires with me now—ready for your signature. Would it trouble you too much if I came across to your office right away so that we can get the whole thing finally tied up?'

I crossed my fingers in silent hope. There was a long pause at the other end of the line. After several seconds I thought I'd been cut off—then I heard my friend take a deep breath.

'Och well now, I see by my watch it's a quarter to ten. I'll meet you in Maloney's pub at ten o'clock and we can get everything signed up there.'

I wasted no time in getting down to Maloney's and almost on the stroke of ten he entered the bar. In due course the document was signed although by the time this formality was completed there were more than just a few Guinness stains on the paper.

On the civil aviation side Aer Lingus, like their military counterpart the Irish Air Corps, had run down rather badly during the war years. They were reduced to one old Douglas D.C.3 and a De Havilland D.H.86. Once again Archie Boyd had started negotiations going on behalf of the Eire Government for them to purchase several Vickers Viking aircraft. My own opinion was that they would have been more sensible going after something cheaper and although I suggested this I could see their hearts were set on obtaining some sophisticated aircraft.

I mentioned that it would be relatively easy to buy a number of Dakotas at as low a figure as two or three thousand pounds each, due to the number that had suddenly come on the market. Although I suggested that it would be a sound proposition to build up a large fleet of these and operate a non-bookable service between Dublin and London, because of their monopoly on this route, they still did not waver.

The Vikings arrived and were soon in operation, but they were costly aircraft to operate on such a short journey and eventually Aer Lingus decided to get rid of them in order to cut their operating losses. When their fleet was building up they seconded quite a number of pilots from B.O.A.C. and B.E.A. Among those who came over was Captain O. P. Jones, the well-known bearded captain of the ex-Imperial Airways days.

Unfortunately he and Jack Kelly Rogers, one of the leading Aer Lingus figures at the time, with whom I still keep in touch, did not hit it off together, and O.P. left soon after. Captain Neville Stack, another well-known pre-war aviator also joined the company about this time—so there was a wealth of experience for them to draw on.

Mr. Eamonn de Valera, who was Prime Minister of Eire, took a great interest in all aviation matters and after several talks with him I could see he was keen on earning prestige for his country by entering the field of trans-Atlantic flying. The best aircraft for long hauls at this time was the Lockheed Constellation and arrangements were made for three to be bought for Aerlinte Eireann, the holding company for Aer Lingus and the other charter companies which had started operations.

This venture into what was fast becoming a highly-competitive field proved too much for their capabilities; they had neither the experience nor the financial backing to put the giant Constellations straight on to the trans-Atlantic runs. To begin with, in order to get some use out of them the Constellations flew the Dublin–London route which was a highly uneconomical way of doing things although it was an extremely comfortable way of travelling. I had several free trips from Aer Lingus on the flight deck of the Constellations and on one occasion actually piloted the aircraft on a flight from London, much to the consternation of at least one bona fide passenger who looked into the flight deck on the way over.

Unfortunately before there was sufficient time to get new routes planned and put into operation de Valera's Fianna Fail

Party was ousted in the 1948 General Election by Mr. John Costello's Fine Gael. One of the first decisions taken by Mr. Costello, the new Prime Minister, was to abandon the plans for trans-Atlantic flying and to have the three Constellations withdrawn from service.

Immediately a hunt for prospective buyers got under way—everyone being eager to get the transaction completed as speedily as possible, with the minimum loss of face and hard cash. B.O.A.C. were heavily committed to many world-wide routes and eager to obtain Constellations as their main prestige aircraft. Word was passed on to them that Aer Lingus had three which were readily available and the Corporation jumped at the chance as there was a considerable waiting period for new Constellations from the Lockheed factories.

Although they had to pay a considerable amount of money to the Eire Government they were happy to do so because it meant they did not have to expend dollars. In fact the politicians in Eire were jubilant about the success of the entire transaction—they had managed to sell their Constellations for considerably more than they had paid for them in the first place.

Throughout my stay in Eire, Margaret and I lived in a delightful house at Glenageary on the hill above the harbour at Dunlaoghaire. One morning while sitting at breakfast my boss, the Ambassador, Lord Rugby, who had been Sir John Maffey, an erstwhile Governor-General of the Sudan, rang me up to ask if I had read the morning papers.

'No,' I replied, although still trying to sound knowledgeable despite this lapse on my part.

'There's been a shipwreck just off the mouth of the Liffey,' he informed me. As he spoke I wondered what this had to do with the Air Attaché.

The Ambassador continued: 'It's a Norwegian ship—the *Bolivar*—and she went aground on the Kish, a rather treacherous sandbank. As she was in danger of breaking up the passengers and crew were taken ashore in a lifeboat.'

'I see,' I mused thoughtfully, still not really seeing the point of this early morning telephone call.

F

'One of the passengers is Lord Mountevans, better known to you, perhaps, as Admiral Evans of the *Broke*. As far as I can ascertain Lord Mountevans and his party have been taken to one of the hotels in Dunlaoghaire. Could you go down and see if you can be of any assistance?'

Leaving uneaten what remained of my breakfast I drove down to the hotel. There, I found Lord Mountevans sitting in the lounge wearing the hotel porter's coat over the few items of clothing he had been able to salvage before being taken aboard the lifeboat. Despite his ordeal he looked remarkably fit and active although he was a man of almost seventy. When I introduced myself he got to his feet, stretched out his hand and allowed a broad smile to pass over his craggy face.

'This is a hell of an undignified way for a British Admiral to arrive on foreign soil,' was his opening gambit.

Sitting with him were his wife, brother-in-law, sister-in-law and niece who had all been passengers with him on the ill-fated *Bolivar*. The Admiral told me that the *Bolivar* had been returning from South America to Norway on her maiden voyage. Her last port of call before setting out on the final stage of the journey was to have been Dublin, ten miles along the coast.

Both the Ambassador and I were able to help Admiral Mountevans and his friends considerably. I drove them into Dublin so that they could purchase new clothing. His brother-in-law, Trygve Andvord, had been slightly injured when the rescuers were getting him off the *Bolivar* into the lifeboat and was taken to a hospital. He remained confined there for over a week and during this time I was able to use my Anson to take the Admiral for several trips over the stranded ship.

Although we both hoped there might be some chance of its being refloated, the relentless pounding of the sea drove her deeper and deeper on to the sandbank until eventually she broke her back and split into two parts. The Admiral was extremely worried about all the luggage he had been forced to abandon because in it were many of his prized possessions, among them the numerous war medals and decorations with which he had been honoured. Fortunately, these were among some of the items salvaged, but quite a number were badly damaged by the salt water.

Even as Lord Mountevans had been scrambling to safety in the middle of the night there had been several things he had snatched and brought with him to safety. One of these was a package containing several copies of his autobiography, *Adventurous Life*, which his publishers, Hutchinson, had sent to him prior to its release. Before he left for Norway he signed one of the books and presented it to me. Each time I look at it on my bookshelves and see the faint traces of sea spray where it marked the cover on that stormy night I am reminded of a wonderful man who must have been a tremendous inspiration to those who served under him when Britain was at war. He was the kind of man who left behind the stamp of his personality, wherever he went.

In March, 1948, I said goodbye to my Irish friends and set off for Air Ministry to take up a post in the Department of the Air Member for Personnel. In the main my duties consisted of looking after the careers and postings of all General Duties Wing Commanders—a job which was known throughout the Service as running the white slave traffic for men. It was fairly humdrum work although there were certain compensations. Among the other jobs that came my way was to act as the Personal Air Secretary to the Under-Secretary of State for Air—a complicated title, but with it went the proviso that any time the Under-Secretary went anywhere on a tour of inspection I tagged along with him.

Attlee's Labour Government was in power and the first Under-Secretary with whom I worked was Geoffrey de Freitas, who was later to become United Kingdom High Commissioner in both Ghana and Kenya. We made some magnificent and highly interesting tours abroad, visiting France, West Germany, all the African countries, Gibraltar, the Middle East and the Far East.

In the middle of 1949 Geoffrey went to the Home Office and his place was taken as Under-Secretary of State for Air by Aidan Crawley, politician, cricketer and broadcaster. Aidan was fully familiar with the workings of the Royal Air Force, having been a member of 601 Squadron Auxiliary Air Force. He had been flying with them over the Western Desert when he was shot down and taken prisoner by the Germans.

Perhaps the most memorable trip I made in his company to far-flung places was one to Japan. While en route we stopped off in Malaya so that Aidan could make a whirlwind tour of R.A.F. units, and unwittingly accepted an invitation to take part in an organized 'raid' being mounted by the Security Forces against a band of Communist terrorists.

It was September, 1950, and the Malayan Emergency was two years old. The struggle to repulse the growing hordes of terrorists was becoming more difficult and more expensive as each month went by. Despite the tremendous efforts being made by both the military forces and the civilian police there seemed to be no sign of any appreciable effect being made.

The Security Forces had a hard and thankless job in front of them. Even to those who live most of their lives in Malaya its jungle is a place to stay away from because at any one time it can be hot, damp, sticky, dark and full of the kind of creatures most people tend to shun.

So dense were parts of the jungle being encountered by our forces that the only way to break through was to hack mercilessly for long, painful hours with a machete or any other cutting tool of that sort. To those just arrived out from the U.K. and unacclimatized, the sudden transformation from comparative comfort to dangerous night patrols must have been hard to take. Men, more used to pounding parade grounds or city streets, had to adapt themselves to the crunch of the lallang beneath their canvas soled boots, then the rasping of the jungle creepers as they sprang back against the crispness of their freshly laundered uniforms—as yet unsoiled by a hard night's sweat of fear and exertion—and the occasional heart-stopping screech of a nocturnal creature ringing and echoing through the unfriendly blackness must have made it seem as if they were creeping through a hell on earth.

Forays by the terrorists against the innumerable small villages, which are a feature of the Malay landscape, were causing havoc to communications and the general business of winning over the confidence of a populace torn between remaining loyal to the Administration and submitting to the requests of the Communists on pain of reprisals. Often these acts of reprisal were savage and terrible and occurred every so often in order to show the civilian population the consequences of failing to join in the fight against the white men and other unbelievers.

It was a motley lot which assembled in front of King's House, in the capital, Kuala Lumpur, to take part in the organized 'raid'. We had eaten an early breakfast just as the first light of dawn crept swiftly in and allowed the sun to prepare itself for yet another day of fierce and unrelentless superiority over everything else.

Early mornings in Malaya are always a delight. The still air is gentle, almost allowing one to imagine that it's cool. Unbothered by the oppressive heat there is time to take stock of the surroundings; to appreciate the heavy scent of the Bougainvillaea blossom; to hear the last dispirited chirping of the crickets as they relinquish their monopoly on the sounds of the night to the more mundane noises of the daylight hours—the motor cars and the shrill laughter of the gardeners and labourers as they joke together before starting another day of toil. It is a time when one can sit and think, or even walk and think, untroubled by the bothersome dripping of sweat or the unwelcome discomfort of clothes clinging to one's body, glued there by the very perspiration itself.

Despite the nasty things one may have said about the oppressive heat on the day before, the brief exhilarating prelude at dawn is sufficient to banish such thoughts and make one so keenly aware of the glory of one's surroundings that it seems there can be no other place on earth where one would want to live or be at that particular moment in time.

I had little opportunity to appreciate fully the splendour of this particular morning. As I stood in the shade of the surrounding buildings our transport drove up and already the sun was beginning its climb to a place of dominance in the clear blue canvas of the sky.

Aidan appeared ready for the day's activities dressed in a pale mauve lightweight suit, flannel cricket shirt, I Zingari tie and 'co-respondent' shoes, all topped by a broad brimmed Panama hat which he insisted on wearing back to front. It did not seem to me that this was the best sort of gear to wear on a patrol engaged in tracking down and engaging a dangerous enemy. I, myself, felt inappropriately dressed in a Service bush jacket and shorts, but unfortunately this was all we had with us.

Nothing daunted our party climbed into the waiting Land Rovers and set off at a good pace towards Kluang, where a number of terrorists had been reported in the vicinity only a few days earlier. Ten minutes after our departure one of the armoured cars broke down, and after a slight delay we continued with only one escorting vehicle. Due to the lack of armed guards, we were growing more apprehensive as every minute went past. Very shortly we reached a narrow track which led off the main road and disappeared into heavy jungle bordering one of the large rubber estates in the district.

High trees and the sprawling mass of the ever-growing jungle vegetation shut out most of the light, leaving only a partial gloom sufficient to show us the track as it ran alongside a tumbling stream. No one spoke and apart from the steady beating of the engines the intensity of the silence was awesome—sufficient to produce extreme feelings of foreboding in my heart at least.

Suddenly the quietness was shattered. The swift, clean-cut crack of a rifle shot rang out somewhere to our right. There were several seconds while it echoed through the trees; seconds in which both Aidan and myself tensed ourselves for the ensuing fusillade. It was the classic ambush situation. Deep jungle, one shot certain to momentarily paralyse and confuse the intended victims, then in the split seconds when they were still off guard because of the sudden challenge, the main attack. This would continue without a break until either the ambush was a success or the killers realized that for once the tactics had not worked and they were forced to withdraw. More often than not tactics such as these worked to the advantage of the ambushers who used to the full the element of surprise and the density of the jungle.

There was no doubt about it—we were surprised. Our armed escorts paused for an instant, their eyes flashing in a variety of directions as they peered into the dense vegetation on either side and on the far bank of the jungle stream. Then in a flash they were gone, crashing through the undergrowth and we were alone and feeling extremely vulnerable. There was a good deal of noise but surprisingly no further shots. Every moment I expected something to happen—even the sound of a rifle shot or the sudden appearance of a terrorist from the thickets on either side of us would have been sufficient to break the tension of those spell-binding moments.

One by one the soldiers emerged from the jungle and the captain who led them came up to the Land Rover. He saluted smartly and there was just the faint trace of a smile on his face as he spoke.

'Sorry about all that commotion, sir. I'm afraid one of my chaps travelling behind accidentally let off a shot.'

The sound of Aidan and I expelling our breath must have been clearly heard over some distance.

The vehicles were started up again and we followed the track until it stopped abruptly in a small clearing.

'We'll have to walk from here on in,' announced our cheerful captain.

I groaned and swung my feet down to the ground. Almost at once there was a deafening explosion. Quickly, I glanced round as I threw myself flat on the ground. About twelve feet away there was nothing to be seen but smoke and flying earth. All around me soldiers flattened themselves into the leaves and even Aidan was concealing his head and neck.

The noise of the explosion died away and again there was silence; that uneasy penetrating silence which jungles never fail to produce in the moments following an alien sound. Far away among the trees a pack of monkeys chattered with fear and the hoarse squawking of a jungle parrot seemed to announce that the coast was clear once more.

Slowly we got to our feet and dusted twigs and a variety of small insects from our clothing. One of the soldiers who had been nearest the source of the explosion removed a chunk of earth from his collar. The captain was peering with deep interest at the crater left by the blast.

He turned and gave his quick smile of reassurance. 'Cunning devils those C.T.'s. They had a small land-mine planted here.'

As we moved off I wondered how many more such booby traps our Communist adversaries had hidden in the vicinity.

We forced on through jungle that to my unpractised eye looked totally impenetrable. But the soldiers knew their business and found trails here and there where we could force aside the creepers and trailing branches with pressure from our bodies. In some places machetes were used to hack out a path but so quick were those who wielded those vicious-looking knives that our progress was only halted for a matter of minutes on each occasion.

A strong musty smell of dampness hung heavily in the air and although no sunlight could penetrate through I found myself sweating heavily with the exertion. I had also developed an irritating itch on my back and in my armpits. The bare skin on my arms and face was scratched and torn in a number of places where trailing branches had whipped back to snap across my cheek or where bushes heavy with thorns had been reluctant to release their grip when my arms had become entangled in their foliage.

Now and again a quick flash of mauve, scarlet, yellow and black told me that Her Majesty's Under-Secretary of State for Air, the Rt. Hon Aidan Crawley, M.P., was still in one piece although the suit and tie were starting to look slightly the worse for wear. For that matter he, too, looked a trifle exhausted—although any time he saw me looking in his direction he straightened himself and pushed his tall frame even more purposefully through the barrier of creepers.

I was becoming so weary of the whole operation, feeling that such patrols should be left to men who were properly trained to carry them out, that my imagination started to play tricks on me.

I kept hearing alien noises which were in effect nothing more than the normal sounds of small jungle animals going about their everyday affairs, and from time to time visions of newspaper headlines such as 'Malayan Terrorists Wipe Out British Minister and Staff in Clever Ambush' swam into my mind.

It was a great relief when we emerged from the suffocating atmosphere of the thick jungle into a clearing which, surprisingly, appeared to have been man-made. On all sides the jungle looked just as hostile as the part we had come from. Aidan came over and muttered in my ear, keeping his voice down so that our escorting captain would not detect any signs of rebellion.

'How much further do you think we have to go? I never imagined things were as tough as this.'

My expression was noncommittal. 'I don't know,' I answered. 'I just hope the next bit isn't as thick as the stuff we've just come through.'

Just then I heard the sound of a heavy vehicle approaching from somewhere to the left of the clearing. I saw everyone stiffen, momentarily, but although I kept trying to rack my brains to remember whether or not the terrorists had any heavy armour I noticed the captain and his soldiers were not displaying any visible signs of alarm.

The noise of the motor came closer, then slowed. The tortured sound of heavy brakes protesting told me the vehicle had come to a halt. Someone shouted something in Chinese. It must have been a joke because immediately several high-pitched voices, one of them belonging to a woman, burst into a babble of conversation followed by a short burst of raucous laughter. A man—by the sound of things an old man—cleared his throat and spat noisily. The voices ceased.

'Ting-ting.' The clear metallic sound of a bell pierced the encircling trees. There was a clattering noise as a gear was engaged and the engine started to pick up power again.

I wasted no time in dashing across the clearing and into the dense thicket. Flailing wildly with my arms I beat down the tangles of creepers and unable to halt my sudden forward plunge found myself stumbling out on to the tarred surface of a road. I was just in time to see the tail end of a bus disappearing round a corner. On its sign above the rear window were the words, Kuala Lumpur.

'I might have known it,' I said out aloud.

'What's that?' I heard Aidan's voice and turning saw that he had joined me on the road. He had removed his Panama hat and was scratching his head with a long forefinger. There was a perplexed look on his face.

'It's a put-up job,' I announced. 'What we've just come through has been laid on specially for our benefit. I doubt if we've ever been more than a few hundred yards from civilization all the time.'

Our escort had now emerged. It was obvious by the expression on the captain's face that he had not bargained for the unmistakable sound of a conductor's bell on a bus to shatter the painstaking plans that had been laid to give the U.K. visitors a taste of what he and his men had to put up with every other day on jungle patrol.

'Tell me, captain,' I asked. 'Are there any terrorists within fifty miles of here?'

They had obviously chosen our escorting officer for his charm and diplomacy as well as for his jungle-fighting ability. He flashed his honest smile.

'Difficult to be absolutely sure where these blighters will pop up, sir,' he replied. 'That's the trouble with the C.T.'s; they're so downright unpredictable.'

From behind us our Land Rover and escorting vehicles hove into sight around a sharp bend.

'Well, sir,' the captain addressed Aidan, 'I expect you feel like a spot of lunch now.'

I saw Aidan's face crack in a good-natured smile. It was obvious he appreciated the point of the morning's exercise and I knew he was partial to a good joke.

We drove off towards Kuala Lumpur. I felt Aidan nudge my shoulder.

'Lunch?' he queried. 'I don't know about you, but a nice long drink would suit my purposes very well at this exact moment.'

13   *Birth of an air force*

In February, 1956, Tengku Abdul Rahman, the Chief Minister of Malaya, returned from London with the news that he had been successful in his bid to win independence for his country. The Malayan population was jubilant but one wonders whether the Tengku was not a little taken aback that he had succeeded so quickly, for the agreed date of August 27, 1957, seemed to allow him little time to make all the arrangements necessary for a country to assume responsibility for running its own affairs.

Above all, it left little time for the organization of an effective internal security force to replace the British when the time came. But such problems as there were, were lost for the moment in the general rejoicing and acclamation of the Malayans who had called for *Merdeka* (Freedom) for so short a time.

The Communist Emergency was still on and there were considerable numbers of British and Commonwealth forces already operating within the country. This meant that any lack of Malayan forces could probably be covered during a build-up period by those of the friendly nations already engaged in rounding up Chin Peng's marauding bands of terrorists.

This, in effect, was what happened, as the Emergency was to continue for several years after Merdeka Day and the continued presence of friendly forces within Malaya could be justified on the grounds that they were engaged in the support of the newly-born independent country against an external threat, even though the operations themselves were being carried out within the confines of that territory.

Nevertheless the Tengku appreciated how necessary it was to

form and build up his own armed forces as soon as possible, for no self-respecting country could hope to survive long, entirely on the military goodwill of its friends and allies. In reviewing his country's needs in this respect, he considered that Malaya should have its own Air Force as well as an Army and a small Navy.

In the case of the former, six battalions of the Malay Regiment had already been recruited some years previously under the aegis of the British Army, and, although mainly officered by seconded British personnel, were effective fighting units and well on their way to becoming completely Malayanized. Indeed, one battalion was already commanded by a Malay, Lt.-Col. Abbas, when Independence became a reality. However, the Malays had very little experience of Air Force matters when the Tengku returned from that triumphal visit to London.

When I arrived in Kuala Lumpur in January, 1956, to assume the appointment of Deputy Air Defence Commander, Malaya, following tours of duty as Station Commander at Ballykelly, in Northern Ireland, Commanding Officer of the Air Sea Warfare Development Unit and Senior Air Staff Officer at No. 12 Group, I little realized that I would soon become involved with the military growing pains of a newly emergent nation. Indeed, at the time of my arrival, the Tengku was already in London and I had no idea that the wheels of officialdom were already turning to set the train of Merdeka in motion.

As Deputy Air Defence Commander, or D.A.D.C., as it was known, I was responsible for setting up and maintaining an Air Defence system for the whole of Malaya and Singapore on behalf of the Air Officer Commanding, Malaya. Until this time no attempt had been made to set up a radar chain in the area, without which it was impossible to control fighter aircraft in the interception of any aircraft guilty of violating the local airspace.

However, the British Government was also deeply engrossed in defence matters nearer its own shores and could ill afford to spare much radar ironmongery for such an exotic location as Malaya. In any event, only three pieces of the requisite equipment were forthcoming and, as they were all of a mobile type, it only required a few months to site them, set them up and to produce as effective a system as one could hope to have with the limited resources available.

Once this was done, it was then only a matter of keeping the controllers in regular practice to keep the system in good shape and it was not long before I was able to turn more of my attention to another important matter—that of reducing my golf handicap, a diversion which did not go unnoticed by the A.O.C., Air Vice-Marshal W. H. Kyle.

Towards the end of August I was summoned to the A.O.C.'s office situated at the end of a corridor in the long single-storied building on the hill behind the airfield, which served as the headquarters of the Group. The Air Vice-Marshal bade me sit down. There was a wry smile on his face.

'The Tengku is going to need some advice on Air matters very soon and, as you can hardly presume to have a full-time job on your hands these days, I have let it be known that he can call upon you as a sort of part-time Air Adviser, when he requires one!'

I saw my frequent games of golf fast disappearing over the horizon.

By this time, Major-General F. H. Brooke had been seconded from the British Army to become the first G.O.C. of the Malayan Army and, as he and I were already good friends, the thought of working with him appealed to me greatly. It therefore required little persuasion on the Air Vice-Marshal's part to get my full co-operation.

From then on I became the Air Member of the Armed Forces Council, a committee chaired by the Minister for Defence (a portfolio at that time held by the Tengku in addition to that of Chief Minister) and comprising other senior Malayan Army Officers, senior expatriate civil servants from the Ministry, the Secretary of the Ministry for Defence and Finance Ministry representatives.

Its terms of reference related solely to the setting up of permanent forces for Malaya and did not concern itself with matters affecting the day-to-day running of the Emergency—

this was handled by the Director of Operations, Lieutenant-General Sir Geoffrey Bourne and later, Lieutenant-General Sir James Cassells. However, there was considerable doubt in everyone's minds just what sort of Air Force was contemplated, and at my request the Tengku invited me to attend a meeting of the Executive Council—the pre-Merdeka equivalent of the Cabinet.

This, the first of many meetings we were to have, was not without its moments of humour, for when I had been first invited to meet them for the purpose of trying to decide upon a policy for the formation of their Air Force, the initial bids were somewhat flamboyant. The type of Air Force envisaged by several on the Council was grandiose, and, naturally, would have been highly expensive to run.

'Well,' said one member, 'I think we should have some Canberras and Venoms to start with.'

From those of us who knew something about the high cost of operating such aircraft there were a few raised eyebrows following this remark.

However, it was understandable for, to the uninitiated, many of these aircraft were already operating in Malaya in support of the ground forces and doubtless appealed to the political mind as powerful weapons, which indeed did have considerable prestige appeal. When I reminded the meeting that for a start, they were expensive machines to operate and that, secondly, they could hardly be the types required at the outset when the Air Force's responsibilities would appear to be limited to the internal security role, we got down to business.

It had been agreed that the British Government would bear the capital costs of equipment, but that the upkeep, or recurring costs, would have to be borne by the newly-formed Malayan Government. This, of course, brought thinking on to a more rational level and, once it was established what proportion of the national budget could be apportioned to the Air Force (initially agreed at approximately fifteen million Malayan dollars per annum) it was left to me to make proposals for the creation of a force within this budget which would provide the support that

the ground forces would conceivably require when the Emergency was over and the Commonwealth forces had withdrawn
from the area.

There were three principal factors which I took into account
when framing my proposals. First, it was important that the aircraft should be as simple as possible, compatible with the job
they were required to do. This, to my mind, was important,
otherwise the Malayan Air Force would be faced with the need
to second specialist advice from other nations for many years to
come. The sooner the force could become a truly national one
the better.

Secondly, the relentless prosecution of the Emergency had
opened up much of the country previously regarded as inaccessible and a number of police posts had been set up in the interior
to control the movements of the aboriginal population, some of
whom were suspected of giving food and aid to the terrorist
gangs operating in the deep jungle. Therefore the aircraft
should be capable of operating in and out of these jungle strips.

The third factor was that the aircraft should be multi-purpose
and not confined to a single role. This seemed to me to be
simply a case of prudent economics.

Bearing in mind these three points for general guidance I got
down to more detailed planning work.

In a country such as Malaya, where most of the terrain is
covered by dense, sometimes almost impenetrable jungle, the
obvious choice was the helicopter. However, much to my disappointment, I had quickly to discard these valuable aircraft on
the grounds of economy as, give or take a few dollars here and
there, they are four times as costly to run as are the more conventional fixed-wing types of comparable capacity.

The next field of investigation involved the study of the short
take-off and landing breeds. In this field the Prestwick Pioneer
was an obvious choice as the R.A.F. had considerable experience
of operating them in the jungle environment and numbers of
them could be made available for transfer to the Malayan Air
Force when eventually it was formed. As an extra bargain it was
a robust aeroplane and comparatively free from the thousand

and one pieces of sophisticated gadgetry so commonplace in modern aircraft. However, something larger was also required and my attention was immediately drawn to the twin-engined Pioneer—a sixteen-seater—built by the same firm, my one-time employers, Scottish Aviation Ltd. The first of the new designs was just starting to roll off the assembly lines.

A further examination of this aircraft showed that it would fit the bill very well indeed as it was also a strong piece of machinery. It would not take long for either the aircrews or the ground mechanics to master its intricacies. Perhaps one of the most important points in its favour was that it could be readily adapted for a number of tasks. Eventually the decision was taken to place an order for this type and it was envisaged that it could usefully be employed in a variety of roles. These would include short-range transport in a passenger-carrying capacity; troop carrier; V.I.P. transport; air ambulance duties; voice aircraft; bombing with limited capabilities; coastal patrolling and photographic reconnaissance.

The initial order was for six twin Pioneers and arrangements were made for four single-engined Pioneers to be transferred from the R.A.F. to the Malayan Air Force at a date to be decided later.

The next problem was the recruitment of suitable personnel to man the Air Force. A happy solution to this stemmed from there having been in existence for a number of years three squadrons of the Malayan Auxiliary Air Force—one at Penang, one at Kuala Lumpur and the other at Singapore. These units were made up of local youths who gave up their spare time in learning to fly. Each squadron had a number of pilots already qualified up to Harvard trainer standard. Their basic training had been done in Chipmunk aircraft, little two-seater aeroplanes which, indeed, had been the basic trainer for the Royal Air Force until a few years previously.

As my job of D.A.D.C. also embraced the command of these auxiliary units, I was well placed to make an assessment of the potential they had to offer. A number of pilots and ground crews from these excellent volunteer squadrons readily accepted the offer of engagement in the Regular Air Force. However, it was obvious that many more recruits would be required and I made two profitable trips to the Templer School at Port Dickson to spread the gospel.

It was, of course, essential for candidates to have a reasonable level of education before they could be accepted for Air Force training and the Templer School was turning out a number of likely-looking students. This, in the event, proved to be so and several boys were earmarked and graded to await the creation of the force. Two were entered for Cranwell where they eventually did well before returning to their native soil, by which time the Royal Malayan Air Force, as it had then become, was both a going and growing concern.

I was also able to arrange for a selected number of candidates for the ground trades from other schools, industry and the Army to be given trade training at R.A.F. Seletar in Singapore, thus saving precious dollars from the limited budget I was being allowed.

In the interests of economy we had decided to dispense with the chore of setting up our own training schools in the initial stages, relying instead on courses provided by the R.A.F., and later by the R.A.A.F. and the Indian Air Force. Now, of course, the R.M.A.F. is completely self-contained for most of its basic training, but in those early days, money—or the lack of it—was a very cogent factor in all our planning.

And so we progressed through one Armed Forces Council meeting after another with the Tengku always at the helm, taking a lively and constructive interest in all that was going on. By this time, too, I was becoming very wrapped up in the whole business and thoroughly enjoying the experience. Secretly, I was regretting that the role I had to play was only of a part-time, temporary nature. The Air Ministry had already nominated an officer to be sent out from Britain to become the first Chief of Air Staff in September, 1957, and, strangely enough, his name was also Johnstone—and a Group Captain to boot.

Initially it had been agreed that the appointment of the senior Air Force role should be as a Group Captain, but this was later upgraded to Air Commodore rank. I think, too, that the Tengku had got to know me quite well and was pleased to take me into his confidence. It therefore came as something of a shock to him when he discovered that his first Chief of Air Staff was not me, but another character of the same name. It was many months later before I learned that he had made strong representations to the Powers That Be, to be allowed to keep the Johnstone he had and to hell with the one he hadn't.

Air Marshal the Earl of Bandon, then Commander-in-Chief Far East Air Force, told me about this when he approached me around midsummer 1957 to press me to accept the appointment.

'I'll make you an Air Commodore if you do,' he said.

Well, who could refuse such an offer even if one was unintelligent enough even to think of doing so?

In this way it was agreed that I should change my allegiance, as it were, on the coming of Malayan Independence and become a servant of the Malayan Government so long as I remained in the post of Chief of Air Staff. In effect it made little difference to me as I was to continue to wear R.A.F. uniform until I left Kuala Lumpur in August, 1958, as discussions were still going on in Council even then, regarding the details of uniform, and so on, to be worn by the various services.

Besides the question of uniform, which eventually emerged as planned, except that we had hoped to be allowed to go in for a greyer material than the normal type of olive green, there was the most important matter of designing an ensign and national markings for this Air Force shortly to be born. As far as the markings were concerned it occurred to me that we should try to get away from the generally accepted pattern of painting roundels on the wings and fuselage of the aircraft. But much as I wanted this I could think of no alternative.

One afternoon an idea suddenly flashed into my head as I watched Iain, my young son, playing around with his paints. Borrowing the box of water colours and a quantity of paper I started to make various marks with a variety of colours. What eventually emerged was an eleven pointed yellow star—one point for each of the nine states of Malaya together with the two Protectorates of Malacca and Penang—placed on an Air Force blue background, the whole being surrounded by a dark blue square.

Next day I showed my rather amateurish effort to the Tengku who immediately put it to the next Armed Forces Council meeting where, to my delight, it was approved.

The same insignia is still carried on all R.M.A.F. aircraft with several points added to the star in honour of the absorption of other territories within the Malaysian fold. Having agreed on the yellow star as the basic insignia it then became a simple matter to design the ensign by first agreeing on Air Force blue as the primary colour for the flag, with the first quarter displaying the national flag and the fourth quarter, the yellow star.

With this job out of the way General Brooke and I, together with Commander Burfield, R.N., who, in trying to form a Malayan Navy was going through the same growing pains as I, got our heads together to see whether we could devise means of cutting out the seemingly unnecessary waste of setting up three separate headquarters to run the various Services. After all, none was going to be a very large force in the foreseeable future —or so we thought—and there were many aspects which were common to all three.

The Armed Forces Council listened to our plans and agreed that we should tack on a joint headquarters to the Ministry of Defence, to be known as the Ministry of Defence (Armed Forces Division). Of course the Ministry of Defence had other responsibilities besides the military—not least of which was the control of one of the largest police forces in the world. In this way the Ministry of Defence (A.F.D.) as it became known, was created with its offices located in an old British Army compound in Rifle Range Road in Kuala Lumpur.

In these offices the three force commanders got together to thrash out a workable arrangement which, we considered, would be compatible with the economic situation pertaining. Indeed, the situation was far from good just after Merdeka, owing to an unexpected crisis cropping up in the tin industry. This had the effect of almost halving the National Income during Malaya's first year of independence. The R.M.A.F.'s budget was cut drastically from fifteen million Malayan dollars to $9\frac{1}{2}$ million which meant us taking a very critical look at every aspect of the force.

It was agreed that the three Armed Services would be placed under the overall operational command of the G.O.C. Malayan Army who would also assume the title of Chief of Staff (Armed Forces) with Burfield and myself bearing the title Deputy Chief of Staff (Navy) and Deputy Chief of Staff (Air). The higher, or policy making, staffs at Ministry of Defence (A.F.D.) would be integrated and it would only sub-divide at the operational level when parochial expertise required it to do so.

Items such as stores equipment, medical services, motor transport, accounting and personnel matters were to be pooled. The system worked very satisfactorily so long as the forces were kept within small limits but, naturally, as each grew in size and complexity it became inevitable that the Laws of Parkinson should apply, until we eventually reached a somewhat sophisticated hierarchy.

Despite the initial setbacks of lack of funds and the inevitable wrangles with the British Air Ministry over prices to be charged for aircraft and their availability, the great day eventually came early in 1958 when the first Twin Pioneer was due to arrive in Malaya. I had arranged for a seconded crew to be at Prestwick to take delivery of the aircraft at a special ceremony attended by the Malayan High Commissioner in London, Tengku Yaacob, and to fly it out to Malaya. The speeches over, the flight began, to be undertaken in easy stages. However, it was not without incident.

With the Suez crisis very much in everyone's minds, parts of the Middle East were still in a state of considerable unrest and British stock in that area was at an extremely low ebb. Not wanting to have our new toy impounded by some unfriendly state, I arranged for the national markings—which, then, no one had ever seen—painted on to the aircraft, to be covered up and the aeroplane registered as a civil British aircraft for the duration of the flight. Upon its departure from Scotland the registration letters G-ABOL were emblazoned on each side, covering the R.M.A.F. colours.

All went well until the crew ran into bad weather over Turkey where they were forced to make an unscheduled stop at a small military airfield. Unfortunately, too, the canvas strip bearing the civil registration letters became detached from one side of the Pioneer during the flight through the gales and torrential rain. The captain, Flight Lieutenant George Charles, found himself in the difficult position of having to explain to a junior Turkish officer, who spoke little English, how it was that they, R.A.F. officers, were flying a hitherto unknown type of aircraft, bearing a British civil registration on one side and an unknown national marking on the other, from the United Kingdom, which he had heard of, to another country of which he had not.

Flt. Lt. Charles told me later that the whole thing became so complicated and farcical that, in the end, the poor little Turk was only too pleased to give them some fuel and send them on their way. He reckoned he could never have explained the situation to his superiors.

The rest of the flight went smoothly and the Twin Pioneer, the first aircraft of the R.M.A.F. and, for that matter, the first of its kind to be used by any Air Force, arrived at R.A.F. Butterworth in Kedah, in the north of Malaya. There it was given a final check over and a good polish ready for its triumphal arrival at Kuala Lumpur the following day.

The next morning I took the controls on the flight to the capital and I'm not ashamed to admit that I felt like a youngster who has just been given the Christmas present he has lived with in his dreams. A large crowd had gathered at Kuala Lumpur to mark the occasion—in effect, the actual birth of the Royal Malayan Air Force.

The sun had risen high in the sky and there were only small patches of thick white cumulo-nimbus storm clouds drifting lazily by as I made my approach into Kuala Lumpur. The engines purred rhythmically and the controls were a delight to handle, responding easily to the slightest touch. Being such an awesome occasion, not only for myself but also for the waiting officials on the ground, I gave that landing the full kid-glove treatment.

The Pioneer came to earth, as graceful on the ground as she had been in the sky, and I taxied over to the main buildings where Dato Razak, who by now had succeeded the Tengku as Minister of Defence, was there to greet me. With him were Sir Henry Lee, the Minister of Finance, and Dato Sardon, Minister of Transport.

They expressed their thanks to the crew who had taken care of the aircraft on the nine thousand mile flight from Prestwick and then asked for a tour of inspection. We were all schoolboys once again on that day. For everyone it was a dream come true—an idea we had conceived and worked with for so long. Now it had truly been born and at last we were in business. The Malayans could pride themselves that they really had their own Air Force —despite the fact that, for the present, there was only one aircraft.

On that day no one realized that it would face its first major test almost six years later when Indonesia would bare her teeth and spit in the face of the Malaysian people. Only a crystal ball could have foretold that when this time came I would have a first-hand chance to see my baby come of age—as Commander of the Air Forces in Borneo.

14 *African interlude*

When I arrived at Middleton St. George, a few miles out of Darlington, on October 1, 1958, to take command of the fighter station there I found two fully operational squadrons—No. 92, a day fighter squadron equipped with Hawker Hunter Mk 6 aircraft, and a night all-weather squadron, No. 33, flying Gloster Javelins. The latter were heavy brutes and had earned for themselves the nickname of Gloster Dragmasters. However, providing they were completely serviceable with all parts working smoothly, they were pleasant aircraft to fly.

I took advantage of as many opportunities as possible to get into the air again and did a considerable amount of flying with both squadrons. Bit by bit, as new and sophisticated modifications were made to the aircraft, I discovered that the old thrill that had once taken possession of me whenever I seated myself behind a set of controls had started to fade. The fun was going out of flying. In a way, I suppose this was due to the fact that I was getting older and one really had to be in first-class condition —both physically and mentally—to master fully the intricacies of these fast moving, highly sophisticated aircraft.

It was also a time-consuming business. To do a forty minute flight could involve one in practically an entire morning or afternoon of planning and preparation. First of all one had to strip almost to the skin in order to get into an anti-G suit, designed to give protection when the fighter was being banked sharply or pulling out of a steep dive. There then would follow the pre-flight briefing, which was always extremely thorough, and needed careful attention in order to reduce all possible hazards to the absolute minimum. The pre-take-off checks in the aircraft also took up a fair amount of time and then the flight itself which was, of course, the most pleasurable part of the entire operation, although one usually shed quite a bit of sweat ensuring that all procedures and manœuvres were carried out correctly.

Afterwards there was always a fairly intensive flight debriefing and then came the awkward removal of the anti-G suit, a bath, followed by the business of dressing in uniform again. In addition, because of my varied duties as Station Commander it was not always possible to take advantage of flights with the squadrons because of the time it meant I would have to be away from my office desk.

Almost a year after my arrival at Middleton St. George a signal came through to say that No. 92 Squadron had been selected to go into training to take over from the famous aerobatic team, the Black Arrows of No. 111 Squadron. This was a great honour for the Hunter squadron and I decided immediately with Bob Dixon, the squadron commander, that a somewhat different approach should be made to the aerobatic programme by No. 92 Squadron if they were going to take over the role in the finest possible way from their illustrious predecessors.

The first job involved weeding out from the squadron those pilots who were not well skilled in aerobatics. To be fair it isn't everyone's idea of how flying should be done and some pilots, while perfectly capable in other directions, have no inclination or aptitude to throw their aircraft around the sky in all manner of designs and patterns. I never was a great exponent of the art myself and, although I tried aerobatics on numerous occasions in a variety of aircraft and had reasonable success, I was never confident enough to be able to guarantee that if I went into a loop in one direction I would come out of it still travelling in the same direction.

When the selection of natural aerobatic pilots was complete we started the training, using three aircraft at a time. When they were familiar with a variety of complicated manœuvres we added a fourth aircraft which gave the formation a diamond shape. Every so often aircraft would be added either in threes or pairs until finally the full sixteen aircraft team was complete.

On one occasion when one of our newer pilots was going through his paces he made a slight miscalculation during the middle of a slow roll when a four aircraft diamond formation was turning over and his Hunter touched the wing tank of the neighbouring aircraft. Unfortunately, with the force of the impact, the wing tank fell off and struck one of the other aircraft. It certainly was an alarming moment because one way or another three out of the four aircraft had been in collision. It took several minutes to ascertain the extent of the damage and bring them into a normal flight pattern again, but, fortunately, the three machines stayed in the air although they gave their pilots and the ground staff several anxious moments before they were back safely on the ground again.

When Bob Dixon was posted to be Air Attaché in Helsinki, Squadron Leader Brian Mercer, a former flight commander with the Black Arrows, arrived at Middleton St. George to take over the squadron. The wealth of experience he brought with him was a great help and he was able to solve several problems regarding the squadron's performance. The secret of first-class formation flying lies in the implicit faith the members of the team have in their leader. When one considers that in aerobatic flying the distance between wing tips is sometimes less than four feet it is essential to have someone leading who, through his skill and common sense, commands not only the fullest respect, but the complete trust, of the men who follow him.

Despite their aerobatic training the squadron still had to keep themselves in trim as a fully operational fighter squadron so, despite what many people may have thought, it was not all fun and games while they practised their aerobatics. It took the best part of a year to bring the squadron up to a standard where it became acceptable as the Royal Air Force national aerobatic team.

Known as the Blue Diamonds they then started giving demonstrations of their skill, which took them to many parts of the world and earned for them an honoured place in the field of aerobatic formation flying. They were also unique, although we were not to know it at the time, in that they were the last of the big, sixteen aircraft formations to be used by the R.A.F. for such displays.

We had a number of Royal visitors during my stay at Middleton. The Queen, Princess Alexandra, Princess Margaret and on two occasions the Duke of Edinburgh, all visited the station during 1959 and 1960. To help prepare the station for such visits we had a close liaison with the Darlington Parks Committee who really went out of their way to titivate the open spaces. On the occasion of the Queen's visit they really excelled themselves. Row upon row of uniformly parted plants were sunk into the ground on either side of the roads destined for use by the Royal vehicles. After the work was completed the fleet of lorries which had carried workmen and plants was driven off at high speed.

The Queen arrived and all went off smoothly. She admired the plants and told me that the flowers were very striking. In the afternoon the aircraft of the Queen's Flight took off with Her Majesty aboard and hardly was it climbing into the sky than the lorries appeared again, as if summoned urgently. Gangs of workmen spilled out on to the grass and in next to no time the plants were uprooted and borne away to their rightful display centre in Darlington. Needless to say I kept my fingers crossed in case the Queen's aircraft had to turn back unexpectedly.

Situated to the east of Middleton St. George was an old wartime airfield called Thornaby. It had been disused for many years until someone saw its potential as suitable ground for building a factory and work rapidly got under way in developing part of its acreage. It so happened if one was flying in from the east on a due line with Middleton St. George that one passed over Thornaby about four miles before touching down.

Middleton St. George was visited frequently by people from Fighter Command Headquarters and on one particular occasion a Senior Staff Officer decided to pay a call and fly in using his own Meteor. It was a damp morning with a steady drizzle falling continuously. Because of the factories at Billingham, Middlesbrough and Stockton there was always a fair amount of smoke in the atmosphere and on this particular morning the pollution and the light rain had combined to produce something between a thick mist and fog. Due to this the Staff Officer requested the use of the Ground Control Approach system in order to assist him in making his landing.

I drove to the aircraft dispersal area, accompanied by several of my senior officers, ready to greet our visitor on his arrival. A message came through from the control tower that everything was proceeding smoothly and that he was making a normal G.C.A. landing. We could expect him to arrive in one minute's time because, said the controller, the pilot had just informed him that he had the runway in sight.

I peered through the haze and was surprised that I could see no sign of the approaching Meteor. The cloud base wasn't too bad and although the fog hung around in parts, visibility was reasonably good, despite the dampness.

A minute passed . . . then two minutes . . . three . . . four— still no sign of the Staff Officer. Puzzled expressions began to appear on the faces of my colleagues and I strained both eyes and ears looking and listening for any sign that the Meteor was in the vicinity.

Five minutes later our Staff Officer got in touch with the Control Tower again. He had landed, but in a most unorthodox fashion, at Thornaby. Mistaking the runway for the one at Middleton St. George he had gone straight down. Only as his wheels touched the badly holed surface did he realize something was amiss. By this time it was too late and when he finally brought the Meteor to a halt the three tyres were ripped to shreds by the rubble lying around on the surface of the runway. It was a rather shamefaced Staff Officer who eventually arrived later in the day, although all were willing to sympathize with him because his mistake was an easy one to make.

In January, 1961, I was honoured to be chosen to attend a course at the Imperial Defence College, Belgrave Square,

London, and spent what was a form of sabbatical year in company with representatives from the Army, the Navy and the Services of several Commonwealth countries together with senior civil servants from the Foreign Office and other Government Ministries. A course at the Imperial Defence College really is the ultimate in one's academic training and apart from lectures there were also opportunities to visit all manner of places such as the Stock Exchange, shipyards, coal mines and other branches of commerce and industry which it was felt we should know something about.

During the summer, twelve of us were flown in a Hastings of Transport Command to Pakistan and India as guests of the respective Governments.

This trip, which was highly enjoyable, interesting and most informative lasted five weeks, during which time I met many notable dignitaries, among them Jawaharlal Nehru, the Prime Minister of India; Mr. Krishna Menon, General Chowdrey (Chief of Staff of the India Army); Air Vice-Marshal Arjan Singh (who later became Chief of Air Staff), and President Radakrishnan (the President of India).

When the course came to an end I was posted to the Department of Personnel at the Air Ministry and it was during my tour of duty there, in mid-November, 1963, that I was flung headlong into the break-up of the Rhodesian Federation.

My instructions from the Air Secretary were concise. 'I want you to go to Rhodesia as soon as possible to give what help you can to the Royal Rhodesian Air Force in sorting out some personnel difficulties.'

The Air Secretary explained that, as the Rhodesian Federation was about to break up, the constitution governing the Royal Rhodesian Air Force would have to be altered. It had been decided by the Salisbury Government that those then serving in their Air Force were to be given one of four options: (a) to continue to serve on in the new Southern Rhodesian Air Force; (b) to transfer to the about-to-be-created Northern Rhodesian Air Force; (c) to retire altogether; or (d) a limited number of Royal Rhodesian Air Force commissioned personnel would be accepted for transfer into the Royal Air Force back here in the U.K.

My brief was confined only to making selections under the final option. However, it was important that I got to Rhodesia as soon as possible as everything had to be sorted out before December 14.

I would, naturally, have preferred to have flown out by the overnight B.O.A.C. Comet flight which ran daily from London Airport, and covered the journey to Salisbury in about 12 hours.

However, the Air Ministry financiers, ever-conscious of their meagre budget, decreed that as much of the trip as possible was to be done under the aegis of Transport Command. Because of this ruling I found myself on a training flight Comet 2 of Transport Command bound for Nairobi travelling via Gibraltar and Tripoli. It was then planned that I should pick up a civil aircraft at Nairobi for the remainder of the flight to Salisbury. Providing everything went according to schedule I could just make Salisbury in time for my first important meeting, which had been arranged with the British High Commissioner for 10.30 a.m. two mornings ahead.

The flight to Gibraltar was uneventful and enjoyable and we touched down as lightly as a feather. However, as we decreased speed, I was sure I felt the aircraft give an untoward lurch which had nothing to do with the surface of the runway. And how right I had been! The starboard oleo leg had collapsed. Hydraulic fluid was pouring out in all directions.

'I just hope we have the necessary bits and pieces available here to make a quick repair,' I remarked to a member of the crew. He smiled, but Fate was against me for, not only did they not have the necessary bits and pieces but they did not even have the correct type of jacking device to lift the offending undercarriage off the ground. The captain could only signal back to the squadron's base at Lyneham in Wiltshire for the necessary spares and equipment to be sent out as soon as possible.

Twelve hours stretched to twenty-four and there was still no sign of the relief aircraft bringing the spares. By now I was working myself into a frenzy because I could not have been stuck at a more inconvenient place from the point of view of getting an alternative flight to take me on my way.

Nothing seemed to be going in the direction I wanted. However, when I was about to book a passage back to London in the next afternoon's B.E.A. flight with a view to connecting up with that evening's B.O.A.C. flight to Salisbury, the bits and pieces turned up and the necessary repairs were swiftly carried out to our Comet. By pressing on throughout the following night we finally made Nairobi just in time for me to catch a B.O.A.C. flight which deposited me in Salisbury only four hours late for my appointment with the High Commissioner. It was, however, a weary and somewhat unkempt Air Commodore who was ushered into the High Commissioner's private office that warm, spring-like afternoon.

Having disposed of the diplomatic formalities and won from the High Commissioner his approval to deal direct with the Rhodesian Air Force authorities, I immediately made contact with Air Vice-Marshal A. M. (Raf) Bentley, an old friend of mine who had transferred from the Royal Air Force to the Royal Rhodesian Air Force some 15 years previously and who had by now become Chief of the Air Staff in the latter Force. Although my friendship with Raf undoubtedly greased the wheels in so far as the primary part of my job was concerned, it also landed me with another chore which turned out to be a much trickier problem.

As I mentioned earlier, one of the options open to members of the Royal Rhodesian Air Force was to apply for transfer to the Northern Rhodesian Air Force of the future (it had yet to be formed) and, while Raf could cope easily with those wishing to remain in the Southern Rhodesian part of the Force or with those who were opting to go out or to be transferred to the Royal Air Force, he was faced with a delicate political problem when it came to choosing the fellows who were to form the nucleus of the Northern Rhodesian section of the Force once it came into being.

Even in 1963 there was little love lost between those whites normally resident in Southern Rhodesia and their black counter-parts residing north of the Zambesi.

'Sandy, old bean, I would be eternally grateful if you could take this on for me as well,' said Raf cheerfully. 'You realize no doubt that whatever my selections would be, they are bound to be viewed with the gravest suspicion by the people in Lusaka.'

A prompt signal to the Air Ministry was answered by return, giving me the go-ahead but warning me about possible pitfalls. My discussions with Bentley had already filled me in adequately on that score.

However, I went through the papers and the application forms of all those desirous of transferring to the North and did my best to fit as many of the one hundred or so square pegs into the squarest-looking holes in the provisional establishment sheets which had been issued for the Zambia Air Force.

I then borrowed a Pembroke from the Royal Rhodesian Air Force and flew myself to Lusaka to confer with officials there about the suggested transfers. Fortunately, the majority of key posts in the Northern Rhodesian Government were still filled by British expatriates and therefore our talks were comparatively untrammelled by prejudice. Things seemed to be moving along quite satisfactorily—if a trifle slowly.

That evening, as I was enjoying a bath in my hotel in Lusaka, I overheard an item on the local news bulletin, being read out on the radio. Its message made me feel decidedly chilly.

'In the National Council today, Mr. Kenneth Kaunda, the Chief Minister, referred to an alleged visit by a senior official of the British Air Ministry to Lusaka who was visiting the country to arrange for the transfer of personnel and equipment from Southern Rhodesia to form the basis for the foundation of Zambia's own Air Force. This, continued Mr. Kaunda, was entirely unsatisfactory as he was not prepared merely to accept throw-outs from the South. He would require the requisite amount of cash to be made available to him when he and his Government would decide for themselves what personnel and equipment would be acceptable in his country.'

As soon as I had digested this unexpected piece of news I rang up my contact in the Lusaka Ministry to enquire of him whether he had heard the broadcast, and, if so, whether he thought my journey had been really necessary. He, however, realizing only too well the pitfalls of trying to go it alone, as Mr. Kaunda was suggesting, confirmed that he had heard it, but added that all was not yet lost and that no time should be wasted if we were not to lose out in the end. He was clearly on my side.

So, working on the basis of my earlier recommendations and subsequent discussions, his staff worked well into the night to draw up the necessary contracts. At first light next morning I flew back to Salisbury with the contracts in my briefcase, having first warned Raf what was afoot and asking him to make available the chaps concerned. As soon as I arrived I got together those applicants who had opted for the Northern Rhodesian Air Force and explained the need for them to get signed on as quickly as possible. The formalities were completed in record time and I then immediately returned to Lusaka with the contracts duly signed and sealed, handed them in to the proper department and waited for the ructions which, surprisingly, never did materialize.

Maybe Mr. Kaunda had been having second thoughts and was more pleased with his share of the proceedings than he had first imagined.

While in Lusaka, it had occurred to me that accommodation for the new Air Force might not be easy to come by. The airport buildings certainly did not seem adequate to house a head-quarters or even a squadron, while the few suitable office buildings in the town itself seemed to be already fully occupied. Fortunately, I expressed my fears to my chums in the Ministry of Industry and Commerce, for this was an aspect which clearly had been overlooked in the hurly-burly of splitting up the Federation itself.

Wasting no time, I flew across to Livingstone where I was able to earmark enough space in the international airport buildings to house a squadron and a half of whatever operational aircraft were to be based there and I was also able to commandeer sufficient hotel accommodation near by to serve for temporary domestic purposes. In doing this I found that I was only one short jump ahead of the Army authorities, for they too had just begun to realize that there was a shortage of buildings and were also on the lookout for increased living and working space.

Major-General Lea, the Northern Rhodesian Army Commander (designate), whom I later met while serving in Borneo, told me that he often cursed the day I stole that march on him when I got in ahead by earmarking those items for the Zambia Air Force.

Maybe it was just as well I was not staying longer in that part of Africa. As it was, I returned promptly to Salisbury and on to England the following evening. On this occasion I had a most comfortable ride all the way home in a B.O.A.C. Comet 4. Somehow or other, whether or not anyone else was of the same opinion, I felt I had earned it.

G

15   *Borneo emergency*

As I flew to the Far East in March, 1964, to take up my appointment as Commander of the Air Forces in Borneo I knew that the job would be no sinecure. Indonesia was in open confrontation with Malaysia and such was the tension engendered by what had become a war of nerves, that both sides were poised waiting for the other to make the move which would spark off a prolonged period of intense fighting.

In their respective capitals, Kuala Lumpur and Djakarta, Premier Tengku Abdul Rahman of Malaysia and President Soekarno of Indonesia attacked each other with a concentrated bombardment of scorn which poured from their radio stations and newspapers.

Borneo, merely a corruption of the word Brunei, is a most rugged country. The border between it and Kalimantan, that part of the island under Indonesian control, is nearly one thousand miles long. The entire country is covered with extremely dense jungle rising in most places to a height of two hundred feet. Inland there are mountain ranges climbing to over seven thousand feet and all are covered to their peaks with this difficult jungle country—thick undergrowth between the trees, creepers of all thicknesses twisting and turning in every direction and evil smelling swamps where the vegetation decays and putrefies among the dripping moistness shut out from the light of the sun by the tangled foliage of the trees.

There is only one mountain free from jungle—Mount Kinabalu which is 13,500 feet high. However, it poses its own particular problems because of the gorges and treacherous rock faces marking its surface for most of its height.

Apart from a few laterite roads leading from the main towns out to the neighbouring rubber and pepper estates there are no decent highways throughout the entire region, nor are there any railways apart from one narrow gauge line running between Jesselton, in Sabah, to the hill station inland at Kenningau. Until the advent of short take-off and landing aircraft and helicopters, the only means of getting about up-country was by using the many rivers. Unfortunately, these were limiting in the amount of distance that could be covered because many were unnavigable due to vast numbers of rapids.

In fact it was said that the only alternative to, say, a one hour trip in a Twin Pioneer could be at least two and a half months in a canoe—providing you intended to go somewhere that a canoe could reach. It was also said that a monkey could, theoretically, swing from branch to branch along the trees from one end of the country to the other without either touching the ground or making contact with any human being. When one has seen Borneo as I have, it is possible to believe such stories. The jungle country in Borneo makes the jungles of Malaya, no matter how formidable they may appear, look like Kew Gardens.

It was in this difficult terrain that our forces were operating, attempting to contain the Communist infiltrators from slipping into Borneo across the ill-defined border with Indonesian territory. It really was ill-defined, because no one had ever mapped properly much of the inland territories and we subsequently found that, in many places, there was a discrepancy of up to thirty miles between what we regarded as the border and what our Indonesian adversaries believed to be the case.

When one adds to this extremely awkward problem the fact that the troops were toiling in a tiresome tropical climate it will be realized that to serve in Borneo the average Serviceman, who constantly found himself out on patrol, had to be a courageous, intelligent and highly dedicated man if he wanted to see that he came through his tour of duty unharmed bodily and unscathed mentally.

One of the greatest hazards as far as the aircrews were concerned was the weather. Towards noon, due to the heat and the currents of air drifting up from the mountainous ranges, great masses of cloud would start to form. By 2 p.m. massive banks of dense cloud would be floating lazily around and more often than not their base came right down to the peaks of the mountains, and lower, in many instances. There was also a tendency for sudden rainstorms to materialize, their ferocity obliterating great areas of the landscape. If any pilot was caught by such a storm when coming in to land, he needed all his skill and experience to get down on the ground safely. So, both in the air and on the ground, the Serviceman had his problems, but despite these there was a form of grim determination among all ranks to get the job done as well as was humanly possible.

Little by little landing strips were cut out of the jungle, generally near the banks of the many rivers, as the jungle always tended to thin out a little in such areas, and clearings were made large enough to take helicopters. Aircraft had a vital role to play in this particular theatre of operations. Our ground forces were utterly dependent on air supplies for their very existence, let alone any military support which might be required.

Every helicopter, single-engined Pioneer and Twin Pioneer —the only aircraft capable of using these makeshift landing strips—was worth its weight in gold. In order to ease the burden and strain on the crews operating in and out of these jungle strips a considerable amount of supplies were dropped by parachute but, if there was any wind gusting, these tended to blow away from the cleared areas and got hung up on the highest branches of the trees dominating the jungle.

The trouble in this part of the world began in December, 1962, with an uprising in the Protected State of Brunei led by an unscrupulous Communist called Azahari. Its purpose was to form the state of Kalimantan Utara, or Northern Borneo, the name given by Indonesia to the states of Sarawak, Sabah and Brunei. Sabah (North Borneo) and Sarawak had joined the Federation of Malaysia on September 16, 1963, shortly after North Borneo gained internal self-government.

It did not take long for the 18th Division, quickly flown over from their base camp at Seremban, in the Malayan Peninsula, to crush the rebellion, but the seeds of unrest lingered even after all outward signs of trouble had disappeared. President Soekarno was quick to seize the opportunity to harass the Malaysian Government, already in the throes of teething troubles with the new states they had taken under their wing. The Indonesian leader despatched a section of his own forces across the border, maintaining that he would help to free the 'oppressed' peoples of Sabah and Sarawak from the yoke of their new masters from 'Imperialist Malaysia'.

Naturally, this was taken as a direct threat to the validity of Malaysia's rights in Borneo, and, in addition, was a dangerous gesture which, if allowed to flare up, could have serious consequences for many parts of South-East Asia. I am certain that Soekarno chose his moment with care because at roughly the same time as he gestured defiantly towards Malaysia, Indonesia was approaching a crisis point in her own internal economy.

He must have been only too thankful to find any excuse to direct the attention of his one hundred million subjects from the appalling muddle he had created with the finances of the Republic.

Out of this show of military force grew the conflict referred to as the 'Confrontation'. Azahari vanished across the border into Kalimantan where, occasionally, news of his movements reached us through Intelligence contacts, but he never again played a significant part in the trouble.

Madame Azahari, one of his four attractive Javanese wives, did not flee with him, but continued to live in the town of Brunei in a house directly opposite the building used by General Walter Walker, the General Officer Commanding, as his headquarters. She was a familiar figure and would often be seen leaving her house on shopping expeditions, her long black hair, partially covered by a brightly coloured scarf, streaming out behind her in the breeze as she raced along the streets in a scarlet coloured M.G. Magnette.

When I joined the Headquarters, Group Captain Roy Scott

was my Deputy Commander and we found a formidable task confronting us.

Until then aircraft and aircrew had been sent into Borneo to support the Army operations from various Royal Air Force bases in Singapore, but there had been no effective control of them by R.A.F. personnel. In consequence a considerable amount of air effort had been frittered away through the natural desire of the Army to use aircraft, and especially the helicopters, for every military movement imaginable. As a result it was not long before these most valuable machines ran out of flying hours and had to be grounded for routine maintenance and inspection.

General Walker was none too pleased, but soon saw the need for keeping a close watch on all flights—after which we were able to meet all his real operational requirements which were many and varied. It was in Borneo that the helicopter proved, beyond any doubt, what a valuable machine it really can be, because in many instances it provided the only way of reaching encampments of General Walker's troops.

Despite the fact that they were so valuable to our smooth operations we never had more than seventy-one helicopters in Borneo, even when the confrontation had reached its climax and President Soekarno broadcast to his people towards the end of 1964 that he would 'crush Malaysia by cockcrow on January 1, 1965', adding perhaps because he was a trifle unsure of himself, 'God willing'.

Our helicopters came from several sources—eight from the Royal Navy; four from the Royal Malaysian Air Force and the remaining fifty-nine from R.A.F. sources. I well remember a visit by a Major-General of the United States Air Force, operating in Viet Nam, who refused to believe that I was telling the truth that we were managing to cope and contain the situation with such a small force.

'Goddam it,' he told me, 'we get that number shot to hell out of the sky every time we move near the front line.'

Later on, army formations were equipped with small Scout and Sioux spotter helicopters which also did much useful work.

Naturally, I had to ensure that the helicopters were deployed sensibly in order not to expose them to unnecessary risks and I was extremely reluctant to commit any of these valuable aircraft to vulnerable areas for fear of losing them. This in no way reduced their usefulness or efficiency.

They were essential for the movement of our ground forces in the forward areas and for evacuating the sick and wounded. In many cases, too, this was the only way to supply the jungle troops with their rations.

Occasionally, military requirements in the border regions meant the complete evacuation of longhouses, where entire communities lived under the one roof. The inhabitants of most of these communities were simple peasant people, but vital to our own forces because they acted as the eyes and ears of the whole area around their village. When it became necessary to remove the inhabitants of a longhouse to safety Whirlwind helicopters would be sent to uplift them. But, invariably, they refused to move without all their belongings. As these usually included hens, goats and pigs our aircraft began to look, and smell, like a fleet of Noah's Arks. Appropriately enough this type of operation eventually became known as 'Operation Pork Chopper'.

Every second year a massive get-together of all the tribes living in the fourth administrative division of Sarawak is held at Marudi, a village on the banks of the Baram River. The headman, or Penghulu of Bario, one of the larger districts further up-country, was a kenspeckle and highly respected figure. His presence at the biennial celebrations was considered most important by the Sarawak Government—so much so that they chartered a special aircraft from Borneo Airways to get him to Marudi for the event.

I had already reached there and was enjoying a stengah on the verandah of the District Commissioner's bungalow when word came through that the Penghulu's aircraft had broken down and that it appeared that he would not be able to reach Marudi in time for the festival.

Telephones being few and far between in this part of Borneo I immediately sent a signal to Roy Scott at my headquarters in

Brunei with a clear, but succinct, message. It read: 'Despatch immediately one Twin Pioneer to Bario to uplift one V.I.P. and bring him to Marudi.'

Roy got the Twin Pioneer away on its mission without delay, but unknown to both of us a Beverley transport aircraft had been making an airdrop at Bario the previous evening when one and a half tons of galvanized sheeting had become detached from its parachute, making a crater almost ten feet deep right in the centre of the landing strip. However, when they learned that an aircraft was on its way to collect a V.I.P., squads of soldiers stationed in the vicinity were launched into action toiling through the night to extricate the metal sheets from the ground and make good the damage to the strip.

They had just completed their work when the Twin Pioneer touched down to await the arrival of the mysterious V.I.P. Soon afterwards both the crew of the aircraft and the soldiers, now resting after their labours, were treated to a remarkable sight.

The gallant Penghulu appeared wearing an old 1914–18 pattern Warrant Officer's K.D. tunic, a medal of the British Empire pinned on the right-hand side of his chest—a medal which he had won legitimately when operating with our clandestine forces during the war against Japan—dirty shorts, no shoes and, perched jauntily on the back of his head, an extraordinary bashed straw hat with a Boy Scout badge on one side, a couple of Hornbill feathers on the other side and an Argyll and Sutherland Highlanders cap badge upside down on the front.

I can well imagine the comments made by the sweating troops as they watched this apparition walk out to the waiting aircraft followed by his two daughters who looked exactly like true-life images of Tweedledum and Tweedledee. Bringing up the rear of this motley procession were two pigs and a massive goat. The Penghulu and his party either climbed, or were lifted, into the aircraft and, wasting no time, the Twin Pioneer took off carrying one of the strangest V.I.P.'s the crew must ever have been called upon to look after.

I know I was more than a little dumbfounded myself when I went up to the strip at Marudi to welcome the party with Oliver

Heydock-Wilson, the District Officer. He, of course, never turned a hair when the visitors emerged from the Twin Pioneer and confided in me later that, although he was pleased to see the Penghulu and his daughters at the Marudi Regatta, he was even more delighted to see the pigs and the goat as they, as it so happened, were a much more important contribution to the economy of the festival.

Incursions by Indonesian soldiers and other infiltrators, dressed in mufti, continued throughout 1964 and early 1965 but, since the official declaration of an Air Defence Interrogation Zone during the summer of 1963, there had been no known incursions of North Borneo territories by Indonesian Air Force aircraft. That does not necessarily mean that there were none because our radar coverage was hopelessly inadequate, consisting only of what could be provided by two re-engineered wartime mobile radar sets based near Kuching, in Sarawak, to the south-west, and on Labuan Island towards the north-east. However, if there had been any unwarranted flights they certainly did no harm and obviously went unnoticed by anyone who might have passed on the information. Nevertheless, the threat was always present and we had to keep as strict a watch as we could against such a thing taking place.

I knew there were few, if any, bases in Kalimantan capable of operating aircraft sufficiently sophisticated to do any significant harm to us. However, although hazards were few in the air, many of our aircraft sustained damage from Indonesian ground-fire when they happened to stray too near the ill-defined border areas.

In a way my position in Borneo was a curious one when I reflected that I had previously enjoyed the company of General Nasution, the Indonesian Minister of Defence. I had met him on several occasions during my tour of duty with the Royal Malayan Air Force in 1957 and 1958 and again had the pleasure of meeting him while I was attending the course at the Imperial Defence College in London in 1961. On all occasions I had found him to be a pleasant man to know and one with a good sense of humour. It was sad, therefore, to find myself on the opposite side of the fence from him in this troubled era in the history of Malaysia and Indonesia.

One morning, when I was at work in my office in Labuan, to where I had moved from Brunei, I was informed that an aircraft flying from Hong Kong to Singapore had been diverted into Labuan on account of bad weather and that an old acquaintance of mine, Ken Charney, was on board. Ken, at that time, was the Air Attaché at the British Embassy in Djakarta. This was too good an opportunity to miss so I sent a message inviting him to call in and see me so that I could have an opportunity to pick his brains about what was going on on his side of the Indonesian border.

While we were in the middle of drinking our coffee a message was handed to me stating that one of our Army helicopters had been badly shot up while flying in the border region near Pensiangang in Sabah and that the crew had been extremely fortunate in getting back to base.

'Look, Ken, when are you likely to be seeing General Nasution again?' I asked my guest.

'As it happens, Sandy, I have an appointment to meet him in about ten days' time,' replied Ken.

'Fine,' I murmured. The glimmer of an idea had entered my head. 'When you do see him please give him my kindest regards and ask him if he would kindly stop shooting at our aircraft as it's becoming a bit too expensive to cope with the situation.'

At first Ken thought I was joking, but after a few minutes I convinced him of my seriousness and he departed, promising to relay the request.

Whether or not Ken ever gave my message to the General I have never been able to find out, but approximately twelve days after his visit, and two days after his intended appointment with the Indonesian Minister of Defence, something happened which was too unlikely to be mere coincidence. At 3 a.m. an Indonesian Mitchell bomber flew across Sabah from south to north, all the time keeping just outside our radar coverage. It circled twice over the town of Jesselton, causing considerable alarm to the local population, and then dropped twenty-three containers towards the ground.

The mysterious objects floated down to earth on their parachutes, but as there were no troops stationed in the area, it was not until daylight the next morning that their presence was reported to us. A party of soldiers was sent to the site to investigate.

However, the containers were nothing more lethal than empty ammunition boxes. Inside each one was a note, which, when translated, read: 'These could have been men.'

When I was informed of the airdrop and the notes pinned inside the boxes I was convinced that this was General Nasution's sense of humour at work once again.

There is something about the psychology of the human race that accepts that there is nothing very bad or reprehensible about putting a considerable number of soldiers facing each other on the ground and allowing them to fire away at each other with whichever weapons they may happen to be armed. However, whenever anything, be it a bomb, a rocket, a man or even a leaflet is dropped from the air the entire affair escalates into a matter of world-wide significance. Realizing this I was determined that no aircraft coming under my operational command should become involved in any strikes across the border.

On several occasions I discussed with General Walker the possibility of sending Hunters or Canberras over Indonesian territory to knock out known forts or other strong points there, but I had to advise against this course of action for fear of global reaction. Apart from that we would have laid ourselves open to air attacks by the Indonesian Air Force and we could ill afford to have any of our limited number of airfields damaged, in case we could not keep up the air delivery of the vital supplies necessary to keep our soldiers alive and mobile in the forward areas near the border.

I am convinced that this policy paid off, but at the time my attitude caused considerable arguments between the Army and myself. I'm sure they must have regarded me as a proper fly in the ointment and while I did my best to sympathize with their feelings I never wavered from the resolution I had made.

The nearest we ever did come to using our strike aircraft occurred twice when parties of Gurkhas found themselves ambushed by greatly superior forces in the forward areas. On both occasions these gallant soldiers were able to take up good defensive positions and get a radio message through, informing us of their position and predicament.

Both times I despatched a Javelin fighter to the scene and on each occasion the pilot dived his heavy, noisy aircraft directly over the ambush position. He held the aircraft in its dive as long as he could, then, in the very last seconds pulled out while at the same time slapping in the jet after-burner, directly over the heads of the enemy soldiers. The noise beneath must have been deafening as well as terrifying because, in both instances, the Indonesians took to their heels and fled into the jungle leaving the Gurkhas to carry on with their patrols.

H.M. Commando ship *Bulwark* was a welcome visitor, for in addition to maintaining half of its Wessex helicopter squadron ashore in Sarawak in support of our operations, we always enjoyed the wonderful hospitality offered by her personnel every time she dropped anchor near Labuan. On one occasion a crowd of us from the Joint Forces Headquarters went on board for supper and a Sunday evening film show. My fellow commanders, Peter Hunt (Land Forces) and Jim Pertwee (Naval Forces) accompanied me and we were given the usual generous treatment on board. After the main party had been taken home from the anchorage about a mile off shore we three commanders were invited below to have a final nightcap with Pat Morgan, the ship's captain, in his cabin.

As time passed I noticed that there seemed to be an inordinate amount of coming and going by, first the officer of the watch, then the Commander and ultimately by the Captain himself. Also the hospitality seemed to be coming up even more liberally than usual. Eventually the news was broken to us. A storm had sprung up and with a force eight gale and high seas running it was impossible to get the Captain's barge alongside to take us off.

In fact, it was explained, one attempt to do so had almost wrecked his launch. However, it was important to get us off the ship as soon as possible as *Bulwark* was due to sail for Singapore at 4 a.m. It was by now 1.30 a.m. and we agreed it was patently inadvisable for the ship to sail with the three Borneo Commanders on board.

'Would you mind therefore,' said Captain Morgan, 'going over the side on a commando scrambling net and dropping into the liberty boat? In this way the boat will not have to come so close alongside.'

By now we were so full of Dutch courage and bonhomie that we would have readily agreed to dive over the side and swim ashore in order not to cause any more complications for our hosts. We followed the Naval officers up on deck and forward to where the flare of the bow was so pronounced that the scrambling net dropped over the side many feet clear of the hull at the waterline.

In great good spirits the three of us took leave of our hosts and, challenging one another to a race down the net, went plunging down the mesh in a most unseaworthy manner to drop, exhausted, into the liberty boat below, which was pitching and tossing in the mountainous waves. The crew were having their work cut out keeping the boat in position, but once we were safely aboard we swung away and headed for the shore.

Bulwark kept her searchlight on us as we thudded our way shorewards. It was only when we were about halfway across that Peter drew my attention to the fact that, although the three Big White Chiefs were sitting in the thwarts, looking thoroughly chastened after their experience on the net, dressed only in lightweight slacks, long sleeved shirts and ties and in danger of being washed overboard by every wave that struck our little craft, the crew of the launch were done up to the nines in oilskins and lifejackets.

However, we had the last laugh because the storm continued to blow with such force that neither our boat nor another liberty boat, already ashore, was able to rejoin its ship until nearly midday. So much for their sailing deadline of 4 a.m.

When it rains in Borneo, and it rains at least part of most days, it pours down with immense force. Perhaps the worst storm of all came on January 1, 1965, when rain fell continuously all afternoon, throughout the evening and well into the night. Thirteen inches of rain fell in as many hours and every road on the island, other than a short stretch of metalled roadway leading out of the town of Victoria, was washed away.

Five feet of water swirled and eddied round our headquarters and for once I was glad that my bungalow had been built on concrete stilts. The monsoon drains, deep and wide as they were, proved incapable of coping with this excessive amount of rain and it was not long before entire palm trees, old motor tyres, dead dogs, cats and chickens, were bobbing around all over the place. It took days to clean up the mess and even longer to get rid of the residual smell.

One day I found myself flying in a Naval Wessex helicopter from Sibu in the 3rd Administrative Division of Sarawak to a forward operating base at Nanga Gaat. The pilot was the squadron commander, 'Tank' Sherman, and my fellow passenger, the Air Commander-in-Chief, Pete Wickham, who was paying us a visit from Singapore. Because of the exalted nature of our visitor I was relegated to the seat 'down below' instead of my customary one in the co-pilot's place.

As usual when making this trip we flew up the course of the Sungai Rajang in order to avoid having to fly over the ranges of mountains which lay between the two places. Without any warning we ran into a thick tropical storm with the rain seeming to fall in solid sheets. Naturally, Sherman reduced speed until we were just creeping along, sometimes below the overhanging undergrowth and on occasions with the landing wheels skimming the surface of the black, swirling waters of the river.

Despite my faith in Sherman as a pilot I felt fairly alarmed as I sat inside the helicopter's cabin trying to decide how I was going to get out of my cramped position if we should suddenly foul any of the overhead branches and plunge into the uninviting looking water, only several inches below our wheels.

The door was wide open—this was perfectly normal for two reasons. If closed, in the tropical climate the atmosphere inside the helicopter became hot and sticky, and operating under such circumstances as over the dense jungle with the chance of being fired on, one never knew when it was going to be necessary to make an emergency getaway.

I watched the surface of the river flashing past below and winced when a tangle of undergrowth came dangerously near the fuselage. As I gazed at this unwelcome sight I noticed what I took to be a large log floating downstream towards us. As it drifted past one of the landing wheels I got the greatest shock of my life when the log suddenly came to life and made a violent lunge at the rubber tyre. Momentarily I saw teeth snap shut as the wheel passed within inches of the gaping jaws. It had been no log—but one of the many huge crocodiles which abound in vast numbers in the Borneo rivers.

I have often wondered since what an ensuing Court of Enquiry would have made of such a mishap: 'Primary Cause of Accident—Helicopter forced down through being bitten by a crocodile.'

The eastern end of our responsibility—Tawau and the surrounding area—was always considered to be our most vulnerable point, should Indonesia ever decide to launch a full-scale attack. Sebatik Island, immediately to the south of Tawau, had the border running through its middle and the beaches on every side would have been ideal for any force making a landing from the sea. The presence of large numbers of Indonesian landing craft massing around this area lent weight to our apprehensions.

Early in 1965 the indications were that our adversaries were about to make such an attempted landing during the next period when there was no moon. Without delay various defensive steps were taken to ensure that all was ready for the attack. Apart from the troops of the 1st Malay Regiment and No. 42 Commando based on near-by Kalabakan the area was reinforced with a number of field guns flown in from the 1st Administrative Division in Sarawak and the Royal Navy patrol was doubled.

A Shackleton Maritime Reconnaissance aircraft patrolled ceaselessly throughout the hours of darkness probing the sea for miles around with its sophisticated radar equipment. At 2 a.m.

one morning the Shackleton made contact with what appeared to be a fleet of fifty or more ships steaming at approximately six knots towards Tawau. When picked up on radar the fleet appeared to be about fifty miles off shore. Immediately, the patrolling frigates were signalled and the entire coastal defences put on a full alert.

Racing towards the reported contacts, the frigates arrived in position just before dawn.

As the first light of day crept over the horizon all eyes were ready for the first sighting of the powerful Indonesian force. Suddenly someone shouted that he had something in sight. The moment had arrived.

Several miles away a small island of palm trees which had, no doubt, broken away from some near-by piece of land, sailed along serenely, the trunks dignified and upright, the leaves fluttering faintly in the early morning breeze. Our 'invasion fleet' was dead on course for Tawau.

16   Search and rescue

Throughout the entire thirty-one years I had been flying, first with the Auxiliary Air Force and then with the Royal Air Force, I was always more than a little surprised every time I found myself promoted into a new job with extra responsibilities. After all I still felt as if I was being paid, and paid well into the bargain, to do what had always been my hobby. Even in my wildest dreams, some ten or fifteen years before, I would never have imagined myself reaching the exalted rank of Air Vice-Marshal and finding myself in command of one of the most operational groups in the whole of the Air Force.

However, that is exactly what did happen and on September 25, 1965, I became Air Officer Commanding No. 18 (Maritime Reconnaissance) Group. But my job was not to end there. I soon found that I was to wear no less than five separate 'hats' as the additional appointments piled up—Air Officer Scotland and Northern Ireland, Air Commander North Atlantic Sub Area, Air Commander Nore and Channel—both N.A.T.O. commands and Air Commander Home Defences (Scotland). Alas, I also discovered soon enough that there would only be one lot of pay.

The principal tasks of No. 18 Group are to maintain an all-the-year-round surveillance of maritime activities in the North Atlantic and North Norwegian Sea and to co-ordinate and control all Search and Rescue operations using Shackleton aircraft —to be replaced by the jet powered Nimrods—helicopters and Mountain Rescue teams, within the same rough area. To give a clearer indication of the extent of this region it could be fairly described as one running from East to West, just south of the Wash to the Bristol Channel and out into the Atlantic, and North and South from 37 degrees W. to the southern tip of the Greenland Peninsula. I could even claim the North Pole as my northernmost limiting mark.

My headquarters were situated in the twelfth-century edifice of Pitreavie Castle, on the outskirts of Dunfermline, in Fife. There, we shared the well-appointed underground Maritime operations room with colleagues from the Royal Navy. The two main operational bases were at Kinloss, on the shores of the Moray Firth, and Ballykelly, in Northern Ireland, from where most of the Shackleton force set out on their missions while the helicopters operated from a number of airfields located in various parts of the east coast from Leuchars in the north to Coltishall in the south. Other supporting bases such as Machrihanish in Argyll and Turnhouse, near Edinburgh, together with the four Marine Craft units at Alness, Portrush, Holyhead and Bridlington completed the picture.

Although our Shackleton crews kept up their non-stop vigil over the two and a half million square miles of ocean—often flying in dreadful weather conditions, particularly in the northern region, during the long, dark winter days—it was the equally stalwart deeds of the Search and Rescue force which more frequently caught the public imagination. Hardly a day ever went past without one or more of the single-engine Whirlwind helicopters being involved in some form of mercy mission.

These flights were as varied as they were sometimes difficult and dangerous—lifting an injured seaman from the pitching deck of a trawler rolling and heaving in a heavy sea; removing a climber trapped on a ledge on one of the rugged mountains of the Scottish Highlands or becoming involved in such stirring deeds as rescuing some of the crew of the ill-fated oil rig *Sea Gem* which broke up and sank during a storm in the North Sea in 1966.

For this particular effort all three members of the helicopter crew were rewarded. The winchman, John Reason, gained the George Medal, while the navigator, Flight Lieutenant Reid, and the pilot, Sergeant Lee Smith, each won the Air Force Cross and the Queen's Commendation for Valuable Services in the Air.

Not unnaturally I was extremely proud of all the men who manned the rescue services because they worked inordinately long hours to provide this public-spirited service which was far beyond the job they had been established to do. It is not generally appreciated that the Search and Rescue helicopters are available specifically to safeguard the lives of service aircrew operating jet aircraft from the airfields on which the helicopters are based. The same terms of reference applied to the Mountain Rescue teams at Kinloss and Leuchars—they too were established for use in the event of a service aircraft coming to grief in the more remote parts of the country.

Fortunately, the number of incidents involving service aircraft remains low, with the result that the rescue services have built up a reputation for speedy and highly efficient work involving civilians in distress for one reason or another. But it must always be remembered that the helicopter crews and the Mountain Rescue personnel do this work voluntarily and that often it occurs outside normal hours.

Two Shackleton aircraft with special rescue equipment were always kept on stand-by—one at Kinloss and the other at Ballykelly, or occasionally at St. Mawgan in Cornwall. Equipped to deal with a deep-sea rescue the aircraft stood ready to go at a moment's notice while their crews were never far away in the duty crew rooms.

One particularly large and difficult search undertaken by these aircraft occurred during the single-handed Trans-Atlantic Yacht Race, organized by the Royal Western Yacht Club of England, in conjunction with the *Observer*, in June, 1968. A distress call received from Frenchman, Joan de Kat, sent aircraft to search an area almost seven hundred miles out in the Atlantic after his tri-maran *Yaksha* broke up during a severe storm and he was forced to take to a small rubber dinghy. Unfortunately, de Kat mistook his position and as a result the searching aircraft spent over two days and two nights covering an area far removed from where the luckless sailor happened to be.

He was spotted on the third day by the crew of a Shackleton of the Air Sea Warfare Development Unit at Ballykelly. The commanding officer, Squadron Leader John Bullock, was in command of the aircraft on a routine sortie to test some new equipment and was flying well to the south of the search area when de Kat was seen. Survival equipment and a large twelve-place dinghy were dropped and a Norwegian merchant ship changed course in order to pick him up.

When word of de Kat's rescue was flashed out by the news agencies General Charles de Gaulle, the French President, was still grappling with the enormous problems posed by rioting that was rife in Paris and other large cities. Nevertheless, he took the trouble to write a personal letter of thanks to John Bullock for being instrumental in rescuing his gallant countryman. When I was told of this wonderful gesture I arranged for the French Air Force to fly de Kat over to Ballykelly so that he could hand over this unique document and at the same time pay his own respects to the men who had helped to fish him from the sea.

Sitting next to de Kat at a lunch which followed the small ceremony I asked him many questions about the events leading to his rescue. A number of people have accused him of being foolhardy and lacking in sufficient experience to tackle such an arduous exploit as sailing single-handed across the Atlantic in an unproven tri-maran. There may be an element of truth in this, but despite the upheaval that had been caused by his disappearance I was most impressed by his modesty, his considerable charm and the obvious respect and regard he had for the men of the Search and Rescue service who had toiled ceaselessly for nearly three days and two nights to find him in thousands of square miles of angry ocean.

However, it is to be hoped that some lessons have been learned from this cliff-hanging rescue. To begin with—no officially sponsored yacht race of this sort should be allowed to take place without ensuring that all the competitors are equipped with reliable search and rescue beacons fitted to the escape gear.

Secondly, let us hope that more attention will be paid to the seaworthiness of the boats themselves. Several of those taking part in this event were not really fit to tackle a voyage of this nature nor were, in some instances, the people who crewed them sufficiently experienced seamen to tackle the hazards ahead.

Thirdly, following de Kat's rescue, I strongly recommended to the authorities concerned that instructions as to how to get at food, cigarettes, brandy and clothing should be written in large letters on all R.A.F. rescue equipment in English and at least two other languages. De Kat had not appreciated that these much needed items were close at hand when he climbed into the R.A.F. dinghy. He had assumed the attached canisters to be sea drogues.

However interesting and eye-catching were the many rescue missions undertaken by our Shackleton aircraft the fact remained that their primary job was to maintain a ceaseless surveillance over the vast area of the Atlantic Ocean and the North Norwegian Sea. Occasionally a Shackleton would be sent off on a special mission to check up on something which particularly interested our Intelligence people or it would be detailed to clear an area in which our own Naval forces wished to operate. But more often they were allocated areas in which they could carry out their most important continuation training roles so that, at all times, the crews would be fit and competent to take on any of the many tasks for which they were responsible. However, it was surprising how often these 'ad hoc' flights reported surface movements which were of considerable interest.

Starting in the late 1950's the Soviet Navies began to build up significantly until in 1968 it became obvious that the U.S.S.R. were the possessors of one of the most sophisticated Naval forces in the entire world, second in size only to that of the United States. As the U.S.S.R. is very much a self-contained Continental power one naturally becomes curious as to their need for such a powerful Navy. It is not as if the Russians are dependent upon vital imports being brought in by large merchant fleets. No less significant, to my mind, are the very large fleets of modern fishing vessels which abound in the Atlantic nearly all the year round.

It was not uncommon for our patrolling aircraft to sight large Russian fishing fleets of upwards of two hundred ships in each, scattered over the better known fishing grounds of the Atlantic and the North Sea. The positions of these fleets were always noted and reported to the appropriate authorities because, although they were undoubtedly going about their business in a perfectly lawful manner, it does not require much imagination to recognize a potential threat to our security should the international situation warrant a change of heart in the uneasy peace which now prevails.

In fact when one takes time to reflect on the international scene as a whole and on what part British forces could play in it, it makes one realize how dependent we have to be for our ultimate defence on our alliances with other friendly nations. To a true-born Britisher the fact that we can no longer claim to be completely capable of looking after our own defences with our own forces tends to stick in the gullet. However, the vast economic changes which have taken place during the past twenty-five years or so make it quite impossible for any one small nation to go it alone any more. We must make the best of that unpalatable fact.

Our active participation in such organizations as N.A.T.O. has allowed us, therefore, not only to share the burden of the high costs, but to work as a matter of course in operating daily as one large defence team within the overall pattern of our European responsibilities. To a large extent this is the role of our forces today and it is not such a bad thing either.

The representational side of my appointment took up a great deal of my time while I was at Pitreavie and I found myself continually being required to represent the R.A.F. at various functions throughout Scotland and Northern Ireland. Whereas the Army in Scotland boasted one Lieutenant-General, two Major-Generals and seventeen Brigadiers and the Royal Navy one three-star and one two-star Admiral, any one of whom had sufficient rank to represent their Service at official functions, I was the only Air Officer available to represent the R.A.F. Consequently, I had to depend a great deal on my Air Staff to prosecute the operational aspects of my job. Fortunately no commander was ever blessed with more capable or more loyal subordinates than I was throughout my three years in the chair in Scotland.

My secondary 'hats' in the N.A.T.O. and representational spheres brought me into contact with many interesting and delightful people, both in the civic as well as in the Service fields. Admiral Karl Hetz was one such individual. Commander-in-Chief of the Federal German Navy and a co-N.A.T.O. sub-commander, as I was, Karl had been the navigation officer in the *Scharnhorst*, during the early days of the Second World War.

Promoted by Grand Admiral Raeder to the rank of captain he led the destroyer escorts bringing *Scharnhorst* and her sister ship, *Gneisenau*, through the English Channel in their historic break-out from their vulnerable haven at Brest.

Nearer home, too, I met another ex-adversary in the person of Karl Schoenbach who became German Consul-General in Edinburgh in 1967. Soon after assuming this new appointment, Dr. Schoenbach called at my office in Pitreavie Castle and during our conversation I discovered that he had been commanding a squadron of JU 52 transport aircraft of the Luftwaffe, based at Catania in southern Sicily, at the same time as I was commanding my Spitfire Wing in Malta. Many were the times that I searched in vain for Karl Schoenbach's transports as they ferried supplies across the Mediterranean in support of Rommel's beleaguered army in North Africa.

I reminded Karl, too, of the occasion when we used Catania airfield as one of our early targets when we started slinging small bombs beneath the wings of our Spitfires. At this time we had the inflated notion that our contributions with the Spitfire bombers must be having a significantly damaging effect on the German war effort.

'Tell me, Karl,' I asked him, 'did we really knock out your airfield in that raid?'

'I don't think so, Sandy,' he replied. 'In fact I can't honestly say that I remember any raid at all.'

And Karl is supposed to be a member of the Diplomatic Corps!

In a Service such as the R.A.F. and in circumstances such as we were operating, both in peace time and in war, it is inevitable that one meets up with old friends and foes time and time again. Every wheel turns its full circle eventually.

When it does old enmities and disagreements are forgotten, for there is something about the Services—no matter to which nation they belong—which breeds this sort of feeling and sense of understanding.

It is something aloof from politics; it is a sort of comradeship-in-arms among people who speak the same language.

The Royal Air Force may not exactly be where angels dwell, but the mutual comradeship that is fostered from within its ranks makes for a better world in the long run.

Index